FLORIDA'S NEGRO WAR

BLACK SEMINOLES
AND THE SECOND SEMINOLE WAR

1835–1842

ANTHONY E. DIXON

FLORIDA'S NEGRO WAR
BLACK SEMINOLES AND THE SECOND SEMINOLE WAR
1835–1842

AHRA
Publishing Division
Tallahassee

First Edition
Printed in U.S.A

CONTENTS

FOREWARD

BRUCE E. TWYMAN, PH.D.
Author of, *The Black Seminole Legacy and North American Politics,*
1693 to 1845 (Howard University Press, 1999) ;
Editorial Board member, *Indian Voices.*

Scholars, who conduct research on the Black Seminole people, select one of the more controversial subjects in United States history. The genesis of the topic can be traced to the 17th Century colonial power struggle between Britain and Spain. The scope of Dr. Dixons' research primarily covers the years from the administrations of, George Washington to James Polk.

During these years national policy on the issue of slavery and the Black Seminoles, was dominated by Southern presidents for 44 out 56 years. Much of the writing, research and scholarship on the subject have been influenced by this time period; and at times, there has been a glaring negligence in discussing the record of Black Seminoles.

Dr. Dixon consequently believes it is essential to be especially cognizant of the role and contributions made by Black Seminoles in the period of study. To this end he conducts superb biographical sketches on key Black Seminole leaders Prophet Abraham, John Caesar and John Horse.

The issues of race and ethnicity permeate the topic of the Black Seminoles. Writers who take on this very important subject must navigate through delicate racial interactions between Native Americans, blacks, whites and Hispanic people. Dr. Dixon conducts his study with a sensitivity which too often has been absent.

Because of the events and realities of the 17th, 18th and 19th Centuries the Seminole people came to be composed of multiple ethnic groups of Native Americans and Blacks. Even a superficial review of data on the topic covering 400 years suggests that it may not be possible to achieve a solid consensus on the ethnic identity of the Seminole Nation. However, in this study perhaps the key goal and achievement of Dr. Dixon is in his treatment of the distinctions between these groups.

Also Dr. Dixon reviews the existence of various groups of Africans and Blacks in satellite villages surrounding St. Augustine and Ft. Mose. While he acknowledges their origins from many locations, he identifies the, "Kongo" region as contributing the greatest cultural influence.

Dr. Anthony Dixon is a Florida Commissioner for the National Gullah/Geechee Heritage Corridor. This commission was created by the United States Congress to educate and inform the public about the impact of the Gullah/Geechee people on American history and culture. The Black Seminole genesis can be traced to the Gullah/Geechee who escaped from South Carolina to Florida. It is extremely important and valuable to tax payers and academia for him to present his research at this time. He presents an authentic and unique perspective. The study and record of the Black Seminole is greatly enriched by his efforts.

INTRODUCTION

From 1817 to 1858, the United States government engaged in a bitter conflict with the Seminole Nation. This conflict would result in three distinct wars. The First Seminole War (1817–1818) is best defined as an expedition to suppress Seminoles, and Black resistance to the encroachment of the Georgia plantation system in the Florida territory. The Second Seminole War (1835–1842) was conducted under the Indian Removal Act. This war was a result of the American plantation society's relentless efforts to enslave the Black Seminole population. The Third Seminole War (1855–1858) erupted as a result of the United States' attempt to remove the last remnants of the Seminole Nation from their homes in the Everglades. Research indicates a gradual process by which the United States attempted to acquire the Florida Territory and rid itself of the Seminole population, while enslaving those Blacks who had become a part of or associated with the Seminole Nation.

This book examines the involvement, leadership and impact of Black Seminoles during the Second Seminole War. In Florida, free Blacks, runaway slaves and Blacks owned by Seminoles collectively became known as Black Seminoles. Black Seminoles either lived in separate communities near Seminole Indians, or joined them by cohabitating or intermarriage. Throughout this cohabitation, Blacks became an integral part of Seminole life by taking positions as advisers, counselors and trusted interpreters to the English (who were rapidly advancing plantation society into territorial Florida).

By the beginning of the Second Seminole War, Black Seminoles, unlike their Seminole Indian counterparts, were not given the opportunity to emigrate westward under the United States government's Indian Removal Act. The United States government's objective became to return as many Black Seminoles, if not all, to slavery. Therefore, it became the Black Seminoles' objective to resist enslavement or re-enslavement (for many) on American plantations. By examining the origins and cultural aspects of Black Seminoles, this book establishes the autonomy of Black Seminoles from their Indian counterparts.

Research concerning Black Seminoles' involvement throughout the war allows this book to reconstruct the Second Seminole War from the Black Seminoles' perspective. It is clear that from the onset of the war, the United States government, military and state militias grossly underestimated both the determination and the willingness of Black Seminoles to resist at all cost. Throughout the war, both United States' military and political strategies were constructed and reconstructed to compensate for both the intensity with which Black Seminoles fought as well as their political savvy during negotiations.

This book has three primary goals. The first goal is to document the history of Black Seminole society, thus countering the tendency to characterize Blacks as wholly dependent upon Native Americans. The second goal is to examine the Second Seminole War from the Black Seminoles' perspective. There have been several books on both the Second Seminole War and Black Seminoles. However, there has not been a comprehensive book that examines the Second Seminole War with a central focus on Black involvement. The third goal of this book is in essence a culmination of the first two. It is the assertion that the Second Seminole War was indeed a slave rebellion. Evidence will demonstrate that Seminoles in general resisted the enslavement of Black Seminoles. Evidence will also demonstrate that the efforts of the US military to place Blacks in bondage were not only a major underlying theme throughout the war, but at various points, the primary objective. Thus, this book will shed light on the idea that the Second Seminole War was indeed the largest slave rebellion in United States' history.

CHAPTER I

ORIGINS AND CULTURAL CHARACTER OF BLACK SEMINOLES

The earliest recorded evidence of Blacks in Florida dates back to 1513 and relates to the Spanish exploration and settlement of Hispaniola. During this time, Spain declared exclusive sovereignty over land from the Florida Keys to Newfoundland and west to Mexico. In 1526, the Spanish settlement San Miguel de Gualdape (near present-day Sapelo Sound, Georgia) was ostensibly the first colony with a number of African slaves. The Spaniards almost immediately became aware of the potential danger of an alliance of non-whites in Florida. As a result, special legislation prohibited Blacks from living and trading with Native Americans. However, due primarily to harsh living conditions worsened by disease and starvation, many slaves joined the Guale Indians' rebellion and began setting fires to the settlement. The rebellion eventually destroyed the colony. Those Africans who participated in the rebellion were assumed, by the Spanish, to have migrated to remote parts of Florida and blended into Native American communities.

The Spanish would continue to be unsuccessful at establishing a permanent settlement and a foothold in the southeast until 1565, when Pedro Menéndez de Avilés established San Agustin (present-day St. Augustine) among the Timucua Indians. Menéndez was granted permission, through a royal charter, to import 500 slaves; however, it appears that less than 100 actually arrived with the Spanish settlers.

The Guale would continue to resist Spanish encroachment and control throughout the 16th century. In 1576, a major revolt again occurred, which lasted four years. Many of the Guale who participated were killed and 19 of their towns were destroyed by fire. In 1583, a black labor force was sent from San Agustin to the settlement of Santa Elena (present-day Parris Island) to rebuild Santa Elena after the Spanish regained control of the area. Santa

Elena became the northernmost settlement of the Spanish. The Guale would continue to rebel against the Spanish until 1597, when another series of revolts was suppressed. As a result, the Guale settlements, particularly on the coast, went into a long period of decline and were eventually transformed into mission sites. By the end of the 16th century, Spanish settlements, particularly St. Augustine, were operating on a dwindling supply of slave labor and reliant upon Havana for imported enslaved workers.

In the early 17th century, African slaves were in demand and were quite valuable in Florida. By 1606, Spanish Florida contained 100 slaves, of which 40 belonged directly to the Spanish Crown. Spanish Florida would continue to rely upon the importation of Black slaves from Havana. In 1618, Florida officials would again request slave laborers from Havana to replace the dwindling supply of slaves caused primarily by disease, starvation and ceaseless exploitation. Throughout the mid-17th century, yellow fever and smallpox were especially prevalent in the area and deleterious to the health of Black slaves and others.

Spanish authority and exclusive control over the southeast were challenged in 1670 with the establishment of an English colony in Charles Town (Charleston hereafter), South Carolina. Disputes over uninhabited lands quickly developed between the British and Spanish crowns. Both the English and Spanish understood the importance of Blacks in their quest to develop and protect their interests in the region.

Historians assert two distinct Black communities began to evolve in Florida: autonomous Maroon settlements in the wilderness of Florida that cooperated with Spanish authorities in the area of present-day Pensacola and St. Augustine, and a Black settlement called Gracia Real de Santa Teresa de Mosé that increased its importance by diplomacy, trade and information gathering. Three years prior to the establishment of Charleston, the Spanish governor reported the arrival of the first runaway slaves from the English in Carolina. It was reported that eight men, two women and a small child had escaped in a boat to St. Augustine. Although the English both requested and demanded the return of the slaves, the Spanish welcomed their arrival. This trend would not only continue but also increase to the degree that the Spanish king enacted the Edict of 1693, "granting liberty to all [runaway slaves]…the men as well as the women…so that by their example and by my liberality…others will do the same." Both communities established a relationship with the Spanish such that they aided in the protection of Spanish interests.

During the 18th century, the majority of slaves arriving in Carolina came from west Central Africa, including Angola, Senegambia, Windward Coast, Sierra Leone and the Gold Coast. Of the 63,401 African slaves shipped to Carolina between 1733 and 1807, their origins were as follows:

Senegambia 20%

Windward Coast 23%

Gold Coast 13%

Whydah, Benin, Calabar 4%

Kongo 17%

Angola 23%

Runaway slave advertisements and notices in South Carolina indicate that during the 1730s, approximately 57 percent of the runaways came from the Kongo-Angola region. During the 1740s, the percentage of Kongo-Angola runaways increased to 61 percent. Between 1735 and 1765, Kongo natives made up the majority of the former slaves listed in the St. Augustine records of Black marriages.

Black Maroon settlements in the wilderness existed by utilizing a pan-Africanist perspective in the social, political, religious and military organization of their communities. These Maroon communities established close relationships with the neighboring Native Americans. The two communities lived, for the most part, in harmony and provided the foundation for what would later become the Seminole Nation. Their culture was created by fusing various African traditions, which resulted in a pan-Africanist ethos within the community. This type of pan-African culture existed with minimal European interference. These pan-Africanist cultural traits manifested themselves in a variety of cultural forms that distinguished their communities from both Spanish society and Native American communities, regardless of their close proximity. Research has shown that these cultural traits were most prevalent in communication, artistic expression and religion.

The Maroon settlements used an African writing system to communicate amongst themselves, which was created by blending the dialects present in the community as a whole. In time, Maroon communities developed into separate settlements, villages and towns adjacent to Native American settlements. The first noted town was Angola. It was located near present-day Tampa Bay along the Manatee River and was closely associated with a large community, not adjacent but in the vicinity. Evidence, such as a letter from British merchants, suggests the possibility of Blacks inhabiting the region as early as 1772. However, higher concentrations of their society seem to be found in the Alachua (Gainesville, Florida) region. In fact, during the Patriot War from 1812–1814, larger numbers of Blacks were noted as fleeing the Alachua County region after thwarting the attempts of Georgia planters to subdue them.

On the Manatee River, Angola provided Blacks with access to the Caribbean, Cuban merchants and the broader Atlantic region. Also, lines of communication with Spanish officials in Havana were strengthened through Cuban merchants. It was these merchants' records (fishermen primarily) that revealed the name Angola as being utilized to refer to this Black settlement. By 1818, Angola's existence was known by the United States, Spanish and British authorities. In 1821, Angola was destroyed by the United States. Its inhabitants either fled south to the Florida Keys, where they were taken to the Bahamas with the aid of the Spanish, or resettled to the immediate east, just north of present-day Bartow on the Peace River, in closer proximity to Native Americans. This settlement was known as Minatti.

Native Americans who also fled the Alachua County region relocated to the east of Angola along the Peace River in present-day Polk County. These particular Native Americans became known as Seminoles, thus, those Blacks affiliated with them became known as Black Seminoles (a closer examination of their relationship will be discussed in the following chapter). By the advent of the Second Seminole War (1835), there were five distinct Black Seminole towns in which the majority of the Black Seminole population lived. They were Peliklakaha, King Hadjo's Town, Bucker Woman's Town, Mulatto Girls' Town, and Minatti.

Archaeological findings at Peliklakaha provide insight into Black Seminole culture; these findings reveal how Peliklakaha differed from both Seminole and plantation communities. The first example is the non-geometrical layout of the town, unlike the family homestead of the Seminole or the normal layout or linear style of the slave quarters in plantation society. Peliklakaha's length-to-width ratio was larger than that of Seminole communities, yet smaller than the typical slave quarter.

The second example relates to the pottery found at Peliklakaha: triangular shapes on the rim shards recovered at Peliklakaha were not recovered at nearby Seminole sites. It has been suggested that these markings were individualistic creations of Black Seminoles. These markings indicate an African presence, given that identical triangular markings were found on 18th and 19th century Ghanaian pottery. A surface survey of Peliklakaha uncovered a black glass bead; blue, green and clear beads were later discovered. Blue beads were also found on various plantations and in African-American burial sites in North America, including Seminole sites such as Weekiwachee and the Fort Brooke Cemetery.

Although the particular spiritual usage of beads in Black Seminole culture is not known, their frequent usage as adornments, for pouches and clothing, has been established. Throughout the shift from Black settlements to Black Seminole villages and towns, the Blacks maintained their Afro-religious values.

Throughout both Black settlements and Black Seminole villages and towns, shrines and altars dedicated to various deities and ancestors were located. According to the practices of their faith, these deities were fed, while women would extract their breast milk to place on the tombs of deceased children. The dead were buried facing the east. During religious ceremonies and worship services, call-and-response and counterclockwise dancing and singing were commonplace, all of which are traditional African religious expressions.

Known African cultural retentions, particularly in the area of religious expression, seem to confirm a strong tie to West Africa. For example, the act of naming a child was considered a religious matter that warranted a ritual ceremony in many West African cultures. Historical evidence clearly suggests a strong Kongo-Angolan influence in Black Seminole culture, especially in the practice of naming. Although "slave names" such as Pompey, Scipio, Caesar, Primus, Venus, Diana and Daphne were more prevalent among the list of Blacks emigrating from Florida to Oklahoma, West African names such as Dembo, Dindy, Cuffee, Mungo, Juba, Quaco, Cudjo(e), Sukey and Rhina were also noted. Words of Kongo-Angolan origin comprise "approximately 40% of Gullah dialect items" of which the Black Seminole language, Afro-Seminole Creole, is derived. The Black Seminole name Dindy was an African-derived word in the Gullah language meaning "small child" and was used to express endearment between boys and girls. The word dindi is also listed as meaning "child" in the Gullah language.

The Afro-Seminole Creole language is an English-related Creole. It is a descendant or derivative of the Gullah language. Due primarily to the isolation of Black Seminoles, the Afro-Seminole Creole language (ASC, hereafter) has retained to a large degree Gullah terms. In linguistics, creolization is defined as a process by which a new language develops through the interaction of communicators who do not have a common language. In the case of the Black Seminoles, ASC's earliest formations included a creolization of English and a mixture of West African languages.

ASC is considered to be "almost identical to the conservative Gullah of a century ago...but it does not have the non-English sounds which Gullah has." The African influence on Gullah is reflected in the incorporation of Sierra Leone Krio and Mende terms. However, Mende did not have a strong presence in Sierra Leone until after 1800, therefore, Mende words are not found in ASC, as it was formed prior to 1800. Linguistic research indicates that both the similarities as well as the differences between the two languages can be identified. Examples are:

> 1. Gullah: e nuh shum or e ain' shum
>   ASC: e nuh shem
>   English: He did not see her
>
> 2. Gullah: e ain' gwine shum
>   ASC: e nen shem or e nuh gwen shem
>   English: He won't see her

In example one, both Gullah and ASC utilize "e" as the pronoun he, she or it, as well as the word "nuh" meaning not or doesn't in English. In the Gullah translation, there are two sentences demonstrating the change in the language and the adoption of the word "ain't" (spelled as ain'). It has been shown that creolization of Gullah resulted from the infusion of more derivatives from the English language. Example two further demonstrates the adaption of ain' in Gullah, while ASC maintains a closer African cultural connection with an African-based dialect.

For example:

> English: Where did those women hear that you didn't want to
> go to John's house with us?

> ASC: duh wisseh de ooman-dem bin yeddy she humuh nuh
> oin wan' fuh go tuh John house wit we?

> Krio: nuh usie de ooman-dem bin yerry she una no bin wan'
> foh go nuh John ho'se wit we?

In this translation of modern ASC, the word "modern" is pertinent here because the translation is derived from studies of Black Seminoles in 20th century Texas. By examining the Afro-Seminole Creole language, we are afforded the ability to trace Black Seminoles' migratory patterns.

1. South Carolina/Georgia: From 1670 to 1749, both states relied heavily upon West African slaves; it is in this area that Gullah was formed in North America.

2. St. Augustine: ASC is noted among the runaway slaves in St. Augustine in 1699.

3. Andros Island: From 1812 to the mid-19th century, Black Seminoles began to take residence on Andros Island. Today, Black Seminoles live there at Red Bay.

4. Negro Fort: In 1816, Black Seminoles are recorded living tin the northwest area of Florida. The Negro Fort will be discussed later in the study.

5. Guanabacoa, Cuba: Around 1820, Black Seminoles are reported to have begun arriving and settling near Havana in Guanabacoa.

It is important to note that these areas are not the sole locations for Black Seminoles in Florida, but areas where they were highly concentrated and where ASC was highly visible.

In 1739, Governor Manuel de Montiano officially established the town of Gracia Real de St Teresa de Mose (Fort Mose, hereafter) approximately two miles north of St. Augustine. Fort Mose was located at the head of Mose Creek, a tributary of North River, which provided an abundance of shellfish and saltwater fish. Freedmen planted in the fields nearby, while smaller Maroon communities developed in the vicinity.

By the time Fort Mose became an official town, St. Augustine had already earned the reputation of being a safe haven for runaway slaves. Thus, in August 1739, word from Native American allies in the nearby areas reached Montiano confirming that the British had attempted to erect a fort in the Apalachee region (northwest of St. Augustine), but the Blacks revolted, murdered all the whites and escaped. These runaways, days later, would seek directions to the Spanish from Native Americans they met in the wooded areas of Florida. Fort Mose quickly became known as a center of Black freedom for runaways and a village of new converts as all residents received some type of Catholic instruction.

In the following year, Georgia Governor James Ogelthorpe invaded Florida, wreaking havoc on Spanish communities in the territory. Although Governor Ogelthorpe's invasion was unsuccessful, many Spanish forts and settlements were destroyed, including Fort Mose. For the next 12 years, inhabitants of Fort Mose lived among the Spanish in St. Augustine. The small Maroon communities that existed in the wooded areas surrounding Fort Mose were forced to flee further into the woods and joined other Maroon societies or Indian settlements. Research has shown that during this time Florida's Black culture was infused with Spanish values, including Catholicism.

For those Blacks who relocated to St. Augustine, a bond formed between the important members of both communities. Due to the fact that there were always a lower number of female runaways, Black males looked to Native American, free or enslaved women in St. Augustine for companionship. Interracial relationships commonly existed in St. Augustine, whether through cohabitation or formal marriages. For example, there's the story of Thomas Chrisostomo.

Thomas Chrisostomo and his first wife were Congo slaves

belonging to different people. In 1745, they wed in St. Augustine. Pedro Groxales and his free wife, Maria, were the godparents at the wedding. By 1759, Thomas was a free widower. In the following year, he married a widow by the name of Maria Francisca. Thomas' godfather had also gained his freedom by this time; however, his wife and at least four of their children were still slaves in St. Augustine. The line between slave and free was altered and crossed in marriage seldom without difficulties. Mutual obligations were understood and honored by both groups. Many of the Blacks in and around St. Augustine also had extensive contact with English and Yamasee cultures. Therefore, what research discovers is that due to the frequent interaction of members of Fort Mose with St. Augustine residents, those particular Blacks were exposed to outside cultures much more broadly. As a result, more cultural diversity was incorporated into their African-centered traditions. Also, once Blacks gained their freedom, they closely associated themselves with various Indian tribes and cultures.

There were objections to Blacks living in St. Augustine; poor Spaniards viewed the relocated Blacks as competing wage laborers. There is little doubt that racial prejudice also became a factor. In 1749, the new governor, Melchor de Navarrete, decided to rebuild Fort Mose. In 1752, when Governor Fulgencio Garcia de Solis attempted to remove Blacks to Fort Mose, he faced stern opposition. Governor Garcia de Solis reported to the Crown that Black opposition to their return to Fort Mose was not founded in fear of attacks but by their "desire to live in complete liberty." This raises questions as to the validity of historical descriptions depicting Fort Mose as a free Black town.

Evidence of forced labor and forced conversion to Catholicism has caused researchers to question the freedom of those Blacks at Fort Mose. The evidence of acculturation suggests that if these Blacks were not indeed re-enslaved, they certainly did not enjoy the same freedoms. Regardless of the exact status of the Blacks at

Fort Mose, Blacks in and around Fort Mose were involved in a cultural adaptation process that mixed African, English, Spanish and a number of Native American cultures. Archaeological research uncovered artifacts of material culture that demonstrate the cultural adaptation process. For example, a handmade pewter medal was found that depicted St Christopher on one side, while the other had a pattern resembling the Kongo star. Thus, much like their Black counterparts in the wilderness, Blacks who remained in close and constant contact maintained African cultural ties, particularly with the Kongo. Regardless of the contact with larger outside cultures, Blacks continued to develop and maintain their own cultural identity.

In 1763, Florida was occupied and controlled by the British for the first time in approximately 20 years. During this time, the majority of Blacks associated with St. Augustine and Fort Mose relocated to Cuba. All of the inhabitants of Fort Mose were relocated. In 1784, when the British returned, Blacks also returned. However, how many Blacks returned who were occupants of Fort Mose is not known. Fort Mose was never re-established; thus, the Black community of Fort Mose remained scattered. Although the Spanish returned and established control in Florida again, Blacks had begun to foster a close relationship with the Native Americans in the region who had by now begun a new Indian nation known as the Seminole. Black Maroon settlements were established in close proximity to Seminole settlements, villages and towns. In time, they became known as the Black Seminoles. Black Seminoles would eventually come in contact with Fort Mose descendants through trade, thus exposing Black Seminoles in Florida to various aspects of Caribbean culture, particularly material culture.

From their initial arrival in the 16th century, Blacks began to abscond from European authorities and establish Maroon societies in the Florida wilderness. As the Spanish began to establish settlements and control of Florida, Blacks began to increase in number. In the 17th century, Spanish control in the region was threatened with the establishment of English colonies in South Carolina. In 1687, Spanish officials reported the first runaways from the nearby English settlements. The Spanish Crown, interested in maintaining control in the southeast, began to encourage runaways from English settlements and colonies; as a result, two distinct Black communities evolved.

Those runaway slaves who remained in the Florida wilderness established communities and relationships with nearby Native Americans and Spanish authorities. They developed an African-based culture which incorporated Native American and Spanish cultures. Although they lived in close proximity to Native Americans, they maintained a closer identity to West Africa. This culture included material objects such as pottery and object scripts, as well as language.

As early as 1739, fugitive slaves were settling at Fort Mose, located just outside of present-day St. Augustine. Blacks agreed to help defend St. Augustine from outside European invasion in exchange for certain liberties. The protection served three primary functions: to maintain a social and strategic relationship with the Spanish, to maintain the Spanish foothold in St. Augustine and to advance Blacks within Spanish society. The Spanish provided food until the first crops were harvested, a priest for religious instruction and established a military unit. Arguably, Fort Mose was the first free Black settlement in what would become the United States of America. At Fort Mose, Blacks would also create a culture that wove together African, Native American and Spanish elements. However, this particular community was transported to Cuba.

Over time, runaway slaves began to prosper and increase in numbers. Blacks either lived in separate communities near Seminole Indians or joined them by cohabitating or intermarriage (this relationship will also be examined further in the next chapter). Thus, they became known as Black Seminoles, a nation within a nation. Black Seminoles would continue to exist with an African-inspired culture that included a mixture of Spanish, English and Native American components.

CHAPTER II

BLACK AND SEMINOLE INDIAN ALLIANCE

In the English colonies, there is no clear evidence of a mutual understanding between Blacks and Indians. Relationships between Blacks and Indians were defined by necessity. Collaborations were confined to specific geographic locations and circumstances rather than involving a massive collective effort throughout the English colonies. The Spanish colonies offer a different story. From its earliest beginnings in 1503 (a mere decade after Columbus), Governor Nicolás de Ovando of Hispaniola "solicited that no Negro slaves should be sent to Hispaniola, for they fled amongst the Indians [who] taught them bad customs, and [they] never could be captured." Florida's landscape, like other Spanish colonies in the Caribbean and South America, resembled the tropical homeland from which many African slaves had come. For African-American slaves, it represented refuge from plantation society. Black cohabitation with Seminoles is believed to have begun shortly after Seminoles settled in the territory. By the early 19th century, Blacks were a noted part of their community.

The ancestors of Seminole Indians migrated to Florida during the 18th century. Seminole migration would continue gradually over the next 70 years. They began as a mixture of people from the Hitchiti, Yuchi, Yamasee and Apalachee tribes. In time, Creeks or Muskogees would migrate into the territory and cohabitate with the aforementioned groups. Horatio Dexter, a trader in the territory, described Seminoles in 1823, stating, "They are by some represented as outlaws or runaways from the Creek Nation...but appear to have been rather a colony tempted to emigrate by the superior advantages for hunting and pasturage."

The word Seminole first appears in a 1765 English document referring to a band of Indians in the Alachua region. It originates from the Spanish word cimarrones. Indians adopted it as Simaloni.

It evolved into Semanoli and finally into Seminole. By the beginning of the 19th century, this breakaway faction of migrating Indians had assumed the term Seminole for identification. British authorities and citizens alike broadened the scope to include other Native Americans in Florida. Cultural differences developed between Seminoles and Creeks. This was due primarily to the adaptations to environmental changes intrinsic in the migratory process. The distance between the two expanded, thus allowing the Seminoles to create an autonomy that was instrumental in developing their own communities. For example, their villages and towns were smaller and were developed in a less formal arrangement. Also, by the 19th century, they no longer relied on the Creeks for direction. Adopting the name Seminole for identification was also a symbol of the creation of a new tribe.

During Florida's period as a British colony (1763–83), an increasing number of Blacks began to inhabit the region. James Grant, governor of British East Florida, believed that the economic development and overall prosperity of the colony relied upon the institution of slavery. He began to offer new settlers 100 acres per head of household and an additional 50 acres for every White and Black person in the family, causing slave importation to increase tremendously. Florida produced a two-to-one ratio of slaves to Whites. During this period, the average plantation had between 70 and 200 slaves.

As a result, Blacks were either purchased by Seminoles or given as presents. The going rate was 40 head of cattle. The quality of cattle corresponded with the quality of the slave, taking into consideration such factors as age, sex, weight and condition. British officials would strengthen alliances with Seminole chiefs by presenting them with slaves as gifts. Primarily as a result of the influx of runaway slaves, which in turn increased cohabitation, the relationship between runaways and Seminoles was also strengthening; therefore, the Seminoles welcomed runaways as well. In time, when Florida became a Spanish colony once again, Seminoles began to forcefully take Blacks in the North Florida region.

Seminole slaves consisted of both Blacks and captured Indians; however, their institution of slavery was vastly different from both the English and Spanish societies. The slaves lived by themselves in their own villages with little or no supervision. Normally, there were three fields for crops between the Black and Indian communities. A crop was maintained by the Indians, one solely by Blacks, and a joint field in which Blacks utilized the produce as tributes or taxes to their Indian counterparts. In no way were they considered or treated as chattel.

As long as they paid their "tributes," they were generally left to themselves to create both a community and culture of their own. These tributes could easily be equated with taxes that any British or Spanish citizen would pay. Colonel G Humphreys, a Seminole agent, described the relationship as such: "The Blacks of the Seminole Indians are wholly independent...And are slaves in name, they work only when it suits their inclination." Seminole Indians were fully aware of the importance of slaves and slavery to Whites. Thus, the term slave became an intrinsic part of negotiations throughout conflicts with Whites (including the war) as well as a useful means for Seminoles to highlight their strength through sheer numbers.

Gradually, Blacks coalesced into two groups within Seminole society. The first group was the Maroons. This group of Blacks was in the company of Seminole Indians the longest. The second group was new arrivals that resulted from the influx of slaves into Florida and was primarily composed of runaways. During the earliest periods of the formation of the two groupings, the fugitive slaves were ostracized to a certain degree until they had proven themselves to be both loyal and productive members of the community. Gradual acceptance was achieved primarily through marriage and the longevity of existence within the community.

The exact number of families produced from miscegenation

or marriage may forever remain a mystery. However, evidence does indicate that marriages between Blacks and Indians were less common than noted by earlier studies. The practice of intermarriage seems to apply more so to the leadership circles of the two groups and less between the commoners among Blacks and Indians. This would suggest that alliances were predicated upon strategic marriages. There are several examples of intermarriage and miscegenation within the leaderships of both sides. Black Seminole leader John Cavallo was born to a Seminole chief and African or African-American mother. Chief Micanopy had two wives, one of whom was described as a mixed Negro. Seminole Chief King Philip was the father of a Black Seminole, John Philip. The most noted Black Seminole leader in Florida, Abraham, wed the widow of a former Indian chief.

Black Seminoles and Seminole Indians alike shared common practices and principles concerning marriage. For Seminole Indians, before a union between a man and woman could take place both clan elders had to approve. In Black Seminole society, parental consent was needed for marriage. Both cultures practiced polygamy up to the 20th century. Men in both societies needed the permission of the first wife to marry again. He could have as many wives as he could materially support. In Seminole Indian society, polygamy occurred more often within a clan. This was primarily due to the matrilineal aspect of clan kinship. Wives from different clans lived in separate houses, as two women living together from different clans was considered intolerable. Wives in Black Seminole society lived separately. Two women with the same husband would not tolerate living in the same house. Marriage within their respective societies was more commonly preferred by both groups; however, marriages between Indian and Blacks were generally accepted. It is important to understand that marriage or miscegenation between the two did not necessarily represent a direct union between Blacks and Indians within the community.

The most important aspect of social grouping among Seminole Indians was the matrilineal clan, which traced its bloodline to a common ancestor. The clan was the basis of determining kinship, marriage and participation in ritual ceremonial functions. It was the clan's responsibility to defend its members when necessary. Each clan selected either a natural phenomenon or an animal as its symbol. This is not to say that they indulged in a belief in animal ancestry. The usage of an animal as their symbol was a classification device.

Marriage did not secure entry into a clan. However, because the clan was predicated upon the matrilineal line, a child born of a Seminole Indian woman was considered a member of the clan. Therefore, if a Black Seminole man married a Seminole woman, he was not a member of her clan, but their children were. If a Black Seminole woman had children with a Seminole man, then her children did not belong to the clan. For the most part, Black Seminoles were not included in the clan system except when needed for classification purposes.

The exclusionary rules and principles governing the clan kinship system indirectly demonstrate the autonomy of Black Seminole society. No matter how intimate a relationship may be between a Black Seminole and their Seminole Indian counterpart, the former was generally not considered a full-fledged Seminole Indian. For most Blacks, regardless of the living arrangement or cultural contact, the omission of clan identity presented a clear separation. The principles of clan identity undoubtedly played an integral part in the decisions to have Black Seminoles live in separate villages. In fact, Seminole Indians fostered the creation of Black Seminole autonomy by encouraging self-sufficiency. This in turn allowed Seminole Indians to sustain their clan identities.

The nature of the Seminole and Black Seminole relationship evolved into a state of codependency. On the one hand, Seminoles existed primarily on hunting and the herding of livestock.

The Black Seminoles' agricultural lifestyle provided a level of agrarian production that Seminoles came to depend upon for the sustainability of their communities. On the other hand, Black Seminoles were vulnerable to the threat of slavery by an ever-expanding White plantation society. Seminole Indians provided both refuge and protection to the Black Seminole. The codependent nature of their relationship is one of the primary elements of the alliance forged between the two.

By the early 19th century, the alliance between the two had strengthened to the extent that it emerged as a recognizable feature of the territory. As early as 1808, groups of Seminoles and Black Seminoles were seen trading in the St. Johns River region. The Spaniards utilized the alliance to their own advantage by hiring Blacks to trade with the Seminoles on their behalf. However, the most outward display of cooperation evidenced itself through conflict with Whites in the territory.

Despite the fact that Seminoles were purposely moving into more remote areas in attempts to avoid contact with Whites, they had come to the realization that plantation society represented a force that could not be completely avoided. It became necessary to understand as much as they could about Whites in order to negotiate a peaceful coexistence in Florida. Black Seminoles became a vital instrument in dealing with Whites. Seminoles began to heavily rely on their Black Seminole counterparts for understanding and bridging the gap of communication between them and Whites. As a result, leaders in the Black Seminole communities became an integral part of the leadership in Seminole Indian society.

Seminole communities relied on herding, hunting, fishing and agriculture for their existence. They utilized the products from hunting and herding to trade for European-manufactured goods. Cattle, hogs and the skins of bears, deer and panthers were exchanged for rifles, knives, tools, powder, clothes, liquor and slaves. Hunting proved to be more useful for trade than consumption.

Leery of too much interaction with nearby Whites, they primarily utilized the markets in Cuba, the Bahamas and small settlements on islands of the Gulf Coast. The Gulf Coast islands were often populated with ex-slaves which allowed for collaboration beyond just commerce.

The Black Seminole communities complemented Indian communities by hunting with them. Both communities would plant in common and form a separate "Indian field" in which they worked together. This "Indian field" was designated as tribute to the chief of the neighboring town with which the Black Seminole town or village was affiliated. Once Florida became a United States possession in 1821, Whites were infuriated by the Black–Indian relationship. Thus, from 1821–1835, relations between Seminoles and Whites steadily deteriorated.

The alliance between Blacks and Seminoles was becoming more mutual through day-to-day contact; they were beginning to develop a more cohesive strategy against the encroachment of Whites. For example, Whites were allowed to come into Seminole Territory, search for escaped slaves and claim them. However, Blacks claimed by Whites reserved the choice to return to plantation society or remain in Seminole Territory.

When the United States gained control of Florida through a treaty with Spain in 1821, it held dominion over Florida and subsequently, the Seminole Nation. The Black Seminoles had lost their ally in the British with the end of the War of 1812, while the Seminoles' ability to manipulate trade and rivalries between the United States and Spain was all but stymied. Indian displacement became a top priority of the administration of President Andrew Jackson. In Florida, Indian removal represented the acquisition of land and the retrieval of slaves.

According to the <u>Niles' Weekly Register</u> (a well-known publication throughout the Antebellum Period), the region between the Suwannee and St. Johns Rivers was "the finest agricultural

district within the limits of the United States." Secretary of War
John Calhoun was informed by the territorial governor, William
P. DuVal, that "it will be a serious misfortune to this territory if
the Indians are permitted to occupy this tract of country." DuVal
went on to recommend the removal of the Seminoles and their
placement under Creek authority, "to whom they properly belong,"
or their emigration west of the Mississippi River. Calhoun was far
ahead of DuVal. Almost a year to the date earlier, he instructed
Indian agent John R Bell to convince the Seminoles to either join
the Creeks or become peaceable farmers in one area. Seminoles
responded to Calhoun by enlightening him to the fact that they had
been in Florida for 100 years without dispute of their boundaries
and they saw no need to change that. From the Seminole response
and DuVal's letter to Calhoun approximately one year later, it is
obvious that Calhoun's orders to Bell had not resulted in success.

In September 1823, Seminole Indians began to negotiate terms
to the effect that Calhoun's orders would finally come to fruition.
Governor DuVal, along with his entourage, met with Indian
representatives at Moultrie Creek (just south of St. Augustine)
to agree upon the establishment of boundaries that would cede
North Florida to the United States. According to the treaty, the
Seminoles were entitled to a region from the Big Swamp along
the Withlacoochee River south to the main branch of the Peace or
Charlotte River. The United States strategically set the boundaries
approximately 15 to 20 miles inland, denying Seminoles coastland
that would allow them to make foreign contacts, thus keeping them
under United States' control.

The agreement was made; North Florida was subsequently
ceded to the United States. Governmental representatives present
at the negotiations and treaty signing quickly advised Calhoun
to establish military posts around the borders "to embody such a
population within prescribed limits, and to conquer their erratic
habits...[and] further induce an early settlement of the country

now open to the enterprise of [White] emigrants." The United States acquired the fertile soil of North Florida without any major complications, however, the retrieval of slaves would be a different matter altogether.

The objective to retrieve Blacks lost to the Seminoles was created simultaneously with the order to remove them from North Florida. In fact, Calhoun's first instruction to Agent Bell informed him that "The government expects that the Slaves who have run away and been plundered from our Citizens or from Indian tribes within our limits [particularly Creeks] will be given up peaceably by the Seminole Indians when demanded." The disputes over the possession of Blacks, between Seminoles and Whites, became the most prominent aspect of the Indian removal debate in Florida.

Negotiations often failed. This was mainly due to the personal vested interests of Indian agents, who themselves were often slave owners, and the influence of Black Seminole interpreters and advisers consistently present at formal negotiations. Seminole Indians became willing to negotiate terms for land distribution, but maintained an uncompromising position on the relinquishing of Black Seminoles. For example, during the treaty negotiations that resulted in the ceding of North Florida to the US, Seminole Indians were required to list the Seminole communities, including the number of residents. The Seminoles listed 37 towns, including 4,883 residents but, as James Gadsden, a United States representative noted, "Objected to stating the number of Negroes in the nation." Furthermore, Article Seven of the treaty required Seminole Indians to be "active and vigilant in the preventing the retreating to, or passing through, of the district of country assigned them, of any absconding slaves, or fugitives from justice" and return the aforementioned to an Indian agent for compensation of related expenses. Further evidence will demonstrate that the Seminole Indians had no intention of honoring Article Seven.

By the mid-1820s, Alachua County slave owners were estimating that approximately 100 slaves were still absconding to reside among the Seminoles. Black Seminoles were accused of aiding runaway slaves in the hopes of expanding their society. One slave owner ventured to nearby Black Seminole villages in search of runaways. Frustrated by the interaction, he concluded that the exact number of runaway slaves could not be determined; due to the fact the Black Seminoles protected them in a multitude of ways. Governor DuVal issued a letter to the Seminole Indians advising them to uphold the treaty. At the end of the letter, he issued a warning that refusing to give up runaways would result in the military seizure of them by force. The principal spokesman, Tuckose Emathla, replied, "We do not like the story that our people hide the runaway Negroes from their masters. It is not a true talk…We have never prevented the Whites from coming into our country and taking their slaves whenever they could find them and we will not hereafter oppose their doing so…"

Throughout this same time period, legal measures were developed in order to settle ownership disputes. As a result, Seminole Indians did return a few runaway slaves. For the most part they refused to surrender slaves. The principal problem with this law was not the content thereof, but its enforcement by Whites when Black Seminoles were illegally taken from Seminoles. Governor DuVal informed the superintendent of Indian Affairs, stating, "I have felt ashamed while urging the Indians to surrender the property they hold, that I had not power to obtain for them their own rights and held by our citizens."

A second fundamental problem existed in that the Seminole Indians began to feel as though they had no rights in the white man's court. "The Indian, conscious of his rights, and knowing that he paid the money, though incapable of showing the letters executed under forms of law, as he had received none, and relying upon the honesty of the white man, protested most earnestly against these demands, and resolutely expressed a determination to resist all attempts thus to rest from his rightfully acquired property..." The law itself existed in an unbiased nature enacted to secure the rights of personal property. However, enforcement of the law secured Whites an outlet in circumventing the law itself.

The legal measure for settling the ownership disputes ultimately failed. In 1825, Alfred Beckley, a lieutenant stationed in Florida, reported that Whites utilized any opportunity, including force, against Seminoles, "so that the whites might possess themselves of many valuable Negroes." By 1828, there were so many claims by Whites that many Seminoles came to the conclusion that Whites were determined to take them all! It became obvious that Whites were going to utilize any measure to increase their slave ownership. The Seminole Indians understood the importance of slave power in plantation society and now had come face to face with the types of measures with which Whites were willing to acquire it.

The close relationship between Seminole Indians and Black Seminoles implicitly developed into a relationship between Seminoles and all Blacks in the territory. Black Seminoles extended both a welcome and a comradeship to Blacks in the territory. Black Seminoles would often cross territorial boundaries and establish relationships with slaves on nearby plantations. Black Seminoles were also partially responsible for the demise of negotiations over runaway claims. The mere fact that the interpreters in the negotiations were sometimes former slaves themselves presented a problem. Governor DuVal asserted that Black interpreters appeared "much more hostile to the white people than their masters" and they were "constantly counteracting" his advisement to the Seminole Indians. He later reported instances where Seminole chiefs agreed to certain demands but would later balk on compliance after conferring with their black advisers. Whites (both in Florida and in the United States government) were beginning to believe that the Blacks were indeed independent of the Indians. Furthermore, not only were they slaves in name only but they also possessed great influence, primarily because Indians viewed them as comrades in a struggle not inferiors.

Governor DuVal would eventually go on to become a primary instigator in the greatest test of the alliance between Indians and Blacks. As early as 1826, Seminole Indian removal became a serious solution posed by Whites instead of a mere suggestion. DuVal would go even further and advise Indian Superintendent McKinney that "The Government ought not to admit Negroes to go with them…I am convinced the sooner they dispose of them the better."

By the end of the decade, White southerners began to view Indians as potential allies of foreign powers and the presence of runaway slaves among them a threat to the security of plantation society. Throughout the South, state laws were being enacted to lessen the independence of Indians as well as make emigration more attractive to them. President Jackson shared the interest of White southerners and began to urge Congress to adopt a federal policy of Indian removal. In 1830, Congress adopted such a policy and appropriated $500,000 for negotiation of removal treaties. Strategies were devised to weaken the strength of tribes, while pushing them westward at the same time. For example, the policy officially recognized Indian fathers as the owners of land and the heads of a family. The measure essentially weakened the clan and its position in Indian society. This measure indicated the intent of Whites to force cultural changes within Indian society.

For White Floridians, their primary reason for the removal of Seminoles remained the same throughout the years. To them, the Seminoles' presence was a problem. This was largely due to the fact that runaway slaves would continuously go to them and elude the capture of their White masters. By 1827, the territorial government had begun adopting the aforementioned measure to entice emigration and formally began requesting Indian removal throughout the territory.

In January 1832, instructions were given by Secretary of

War Lewis Cass to draft a treaty and arrange the removal of the Seminoles to live within the Creek Nation in the West. As always, Black Seminole leaders were present during negotiations. Whites would continue to claim as many runaways as possible, while Seminoles were still reluctant to relinquish any to their authority. A division among the Seminole Nation was also developing in terms of provisions within the possible treaty. As far as the United States was concerned, the Seminoles belonged to the Creek Confederacy. Neither Black Seminoles nor their Indian counterparts wished to reside within the Creek Confederacy.

The Seminoles had been gradually asserting their autonomy for many years, but the Creeks refused to acknowledge their separate identity. By utilizing their clan identity ties, the Creeks often included the Seminoles in their treaties with the United States regardless of Seminole opinion or the presence of Seminole leaders during negotiations. For Black Seminoles, a reunification with Creeks in the West would only guarantee re-enslavement.

By asserting the inclusion of Seminoles within the Creek Confederacy, the latter would go further to assert claims on Black Seminoles during negotiations. Demands were then made by the Creeks concerning Black Seminoles, thus complicating matters for all involved. Indian agent Thompson advised Governor DuVal, "As it would be difficult, not to say impossible, to prove that the negroes claimed by the Creeks, now in the possession of the Seminole Indians, are the identical negroes, or their descendants...I cannot conceive that the Creeks can be supposed to have a fair claim to them..." Nevertheless, Washington authorities would continue combining Creeks and Seminoles during their Indian removal activities in Florida.

In regard to Black Seminoles, it became quite clear that US policy was only interested in their enslavement. Due to the conditions of the treaties of emigration (which will be further examined later), Blacks would begin to assert objections different from those of the

Indians. Failed treaties and ever increasing hostilities would result in the costliest and deadliest war between Whites and Indians known as the Second Seminole War.

In essence, what we find in examining the relationship between Blacks and Seminole Indians is a cohesiveness unlike any other relationship between Blacks and Indians of the Southeast. All other members of the Five Civilized Tribes included slave codes in their constitution. Creek law frowned upon intermarriage between the two. In 1827, the Cherokees excluded Blacks from political involvement and discouraged joint emigration. The Choctaws imitated White society in the laws affecting Blacks after emigration.

The alliance between Blacks and Indians within the Seminole Nation began with a basic empathy for one another. Seminole Indians understood the urge of Blacks to attain as well as maintain their own freedom. This basic empathy developed into a codependent relationship. The intermarriages and cultural exchange that occurred between the groups strengthened their ties. Much of the collaboration between Blacks and Indians was motivated by the presence of a common foe. The Seminole Nation grew in response to increased oppression by Whites. Their codependency became the key to their survival. They found a way to coexist, while at the same time maintaining their own cultural identity. Here again, because Whites often treated them differently, they were able to retain cultural traits through their own distinct experiences.

Black Seminoles were incorporated into Seminole life in different ways. However, because they were allowed their own living arrangements and encouraged to be self-sufficient, they maintained a separate identity. Black Seminoles gained their Seminole Indian counterparts' respect by becoming trusted interpreters, advisers, wives, husbands, hunters, warriors and field hands. For them, any status among Seminole Indians was better than chattel slavery with Whites.

CHAPTER III

BLACK SEMINOLE EARLY RESISTANCE AND INVOLVEMENT
DURING THE SECOND SEMINOLE WAR

As with any major historical event, the Second Seminole War was the result of culminating events. It would prove inadequate, to say the least, to examine the war without discussing the arising tensions, conflicts and political climate which existed prior to it. Accordingly, time periods previously examined are included in this chapter with emphasis solely on Black Seminoles.

Blacks were organizing themselves with their own leaders in militias since the 1600s. They began to provide military service to Spanish authorities which in turn garnered them recognition from the Spanish Crown. Once their service was formally recognized by the Edict of 1693, they were incorporated into the military. Like other military organizations serving the Crown, black militias had regular officers, systematic training and state-supplied pay, equipment, arms and uniforms.

During the 18th century, tensions began to increase between Britain and Spain, and both sides began to seek ways to destabilize the other in the Americas. Spain, in order to challenge the British, allied themselves with slaves in the English colonies. Thus, Florida became a safe haven for Black runaways. The origins of the development of this policy may be traced back to the latter part of the 17th century. It is not known whether the policy of accepting runaways was initiated solely by the Spanish (without the influence of the runaways themselves) or was simply a result of recognizing that the influx of runaways brought political and military advantages. However, the Edict of 1693 appears to set the precedence. King Charles II wrote to Governor Quiroga in response to the question of allowing runaways to convert to Catholicism, stating:

> To the Governor and Captain General of the city of St.
> Augustine…It has been notified in different letters, dated
> 1688, 1689, and 1690, that eight black males and two black
> females who had run away from the city of San Jorge, arrived
> to that presidio asking for the holy water of baptism, which
> they received after being instructed in Christian doctrine.
> Later on, the chief sergeant of San Jorge visited the city with
> the intention to claim the runaways, but it was not proper
> to do so, because they had already become Christians…As a
> prize for having adopted the Catholic doctrine and become
> Catholicized, as soon as you get the letter, set them all free
> and give them anything they need, and favor them as much
> as possible. I hope them to be an example, together with my
> generosity, of what others should do. I want to be notified of
> the following of my instruction as soon as possible.

The king's letter indicates that religious convictions seem to have influenced the decision to use Blacks for military as well as political advantages over the British. However, when examining the Edict of 1693 in the geopolitical context of North America, the use of Catholicism appears to become the vehicle by which Spain was able to justify the strategic acceptance of runaway slaves. Charles II waited five years before he responded to the letter. He received the first letter in 1688, as indicated in his 1693 response letter. In that time, he was able to assess the importance of Blacks as a tool against the British. During this same period, Carolina citizens (under British colonial rule) made several complaints to Spanish authorities concerning the return of runaway slaves. In response, Spanish authorities promised to compensate them for their slaves but not to return the slaves. This promise was never fulfilled.

It would seem that if religious exhortations were the key element to keeping the slaves, then compensation in some manner would have been a safer and more amicable diplomatic gesture. The king was informed that the British subjects preferred their slaves. The question then becomes: why did it take five years to issue the letter when tensions where steadily rising? During the five years,

Charles II realized that the loss of slaves would seriously weaken the Carolina colony and, in turn, weaken the British strongholds in North America. By issuing the Edict of 1693, he was able to accomplish two goals in the struggle with England. He was able to weaken British power in the area, while also procuring manpower for the defense of Florida. The guarantee of freedom and safety established Blacks as a key element in his defense of Florida for Spain.

The Yamasee War, 1714–1716, demonstrated the impact and future implications of the Edict of 1693. It also demonstrated the strength of a united Black and Indian military force. The Yamasee and Creek Indians had been allied with the British. The Yamasees assisted the British in capturing Apalachee Indians for the purpose of Indian slave trading. Throughout their relationship with the British, the Yamasees were involved in trading with British subjects. In time, the Yamasees created a debt with British traders which in turn caused the latter to seize Yamasees as slaves for repayment of debt. In doing so, they began a war in which Yamasees, Creeks and Apalachees attacked the South Carolina colony. Many slaves joined the war against the British.

By 1716, the British, along with those Indians still loyal to them, defeated the Yamasees and their allies. The defeated (along with their allies) left South Carolina and headed to St. Augustine where they would not only be safe, but would also be afforded the chance to ally themselves with a stronger force against the British. Although there was an established underground railroad of Africans into St. Augustine even before the Yamasee War, the war represented an open alliance between the Spanish and Black slaves in British colonial North America. During the war, the Spanish supported the hit-and-run tactics of the united front against the British in order to destroy them in the Southeast. Though the effort was thwarted, the Yamasee War strengthened the political goals of the Edict of 1693 for the Spanish, while helping to create the dynamics of the Seminole and Black Seminole alliance. The Stono Rebellion, in 1739, caused an influx of Blacks into Florida. Furthermore, they established the military bond between Indians and Blacks in resistance to slavery.

From 1717 to 1740, Blacks established themselves in Spanish Florida through military service to the Crown. Despite the Edict of 1693, many Blacks found themselves in either slavery or indentured servitude in Spanish Florida. Consequently, it is during this period that the first primary Black leader emerged. It is important to note that at this particular time these groups were not known or recognized as Black Seminoles, however, they did represent the basis for Black freedom in Florida.

Francisco Menendez was a Mandingo runaway in South Carolina who had fought in the Yamasee War and fled to Florida. In Florida, Menendez was again in a condition similar to indentured servitude. He went on to become the leader of the Black militia in St. Augustine. He established himself by helping to defeat the British in a 1728 attack. In 1737, his petition, The Runaway Negroes from English Plantations to the Crown, was accepted by Spanish authorities. In this petition, Menendez urged the authorities to adhere to the Edict of 1693 and grant Blacks full freedom and appoint Menendez as the governor of Fort Mose. For Blacks, it would demonstrate that military service was the key to securing their freedom. This concept would prove effective throughout the Seminole wars.

In 1739, South Carolina leaders received a declaration of war from England against Spain. Tensions between England and Spain had increased to the point where negotiations and treaties had become null and void. The British cited the edicts of 1693 and 1738 as policies directly aimed at destroying the colony of South Carolina. The following year, the British launched their largest assault on the Spanish in North America, with St. Augustine being the primary point of assault.

During the assault, the Black militia was relocated to St. Augustine in defense of the city. The British occupied the abandoned Fort Mose and utilized it as a point of attack on St. Augustine. On June 15, 1740, the Black militia, along with a group of Indians under the command of Menendez, attacked the British at Fort Mose. In less than one month, the British forces evacuated the fort. From this particular point onward, the Spanish would be largely dependent on auxiliary forces for protection in Florida. Menendez utilized his position and the dependence of Spain on the Black militia to his advantage. By 1752, Fort Mose was completely rebuilt and re-occupied by Blacks.

For the next decade, the Black militia would continue to provide service to the Spanish Crown, defending St. Augustine in exchange for freedom and land for Blacks in and around Fort Mose. Runaways from South Carolina would continue to increase the Black population in the region. During this time, members of the Yamasee, Creeks, Apalachee, Yuchi and Hitchiti tribes were beginning to create the Seminole Nation. The geopolitical and military struggles among the British, Spanish and French were beginning to reshape North America. By 1763, the Treaty of Paris had ended the conflict between the British and Spanish in Florida, and Florida was ceded to the British. The lives of Blacks and Indians alike would be transformed forever. The loss of a powerful ally in Spain would cause them to begin to forge a bond that became the essence of their survival.

British dominion over the Florida Territory lasted for 20 years. During this time, military service was all but nonexistent. With the relocation of the majority of the Black militia from Fort Mose to Cuba, those Blacks who remained began to cohabitate with other Blacks in the wilderness, including runaway slaves who were still absconding from South Carolina and newly-colonized Georgia, along with Indians. The Seminoles were now spreading out across Central and North Florida. They were no longer concentrated around St. Augustine. Large bands created a society in the Alachua and Pensacola regions. This was primarily due to their cohabitation with a large number of Creeks who became disenchanted with the Creek Nation and sought independence. It is during this period that many Blacks, primarily runaways, began to create villages in close proximity to the Seminoles.

In 1783, the geopolitical climate would again change. The Treaty of Paris, which ended the American Revolution, ceded Florida back to Spain. Although Spain sought to restore Spanish Florida to its previous state, Spaniards found themselves a minority in the territory. A number of South Carolina and Georgia planters had created a plantation society in East Florida surrounding St. Augustine. The Blacks and Indians who remained in East Florida had now created a society that included traits of Spanish culture. Those free Blacks and Indians who were closely associated with the Spanish through Fort Mose in St. Augustine seem to have remained in the Caribbean. While there is no evidence of their return, Black militias resurfaced, with the Seminoles as their primary ally. From this point onward, Black military leadership evolved into Black Seminole leadership.

As with the British, Americans viewed the edicts of 1693 and 1783 as a direct threat to plantation society. Although the edicts were repealed, Spanish authorities made no attempts to return runaway slaves. Secretary of State for the Continental Congress John Jay informed Thomas Jefferson that Seminoles were wreaking havoc on the state of Georgia and that something had to be done. The Spanish position in Florida was weak at best. Alachua Seminoles represented a buffer between the United States and Spanish Florida, therefore Spanish authorities supported the Seminoles by granting them land and money to prosper in the region. All inhabitants profited through trade. For Spaniards, to adhere to any sanction against the Seminoles was to inevitably lose a valued ally, thus making the territory quite vulnerable to seizure. To return any runaway slaves would ultimately have the same consequences. Therefore, what we find at the advent of the 19th century is the resurfacing of the same tensions between plantation society in Georgia and South Carolina and Spanish Florida.

Once again tensions mounted, such that in 1811, United States President James Madison was given authorization by Congress to use military force to seize Florida. President Madison at this point was in a very delicate situation to say the least. Tensions between the United States and England had also increased to the degree that war was imminent. Madison was careful not to spark violent conflicts with both Spain and England simultaneously. He outwardly admonished Georgia Governor David B. Mitchell for any open attacks against Florida, while allowing Secretary of State James Monroe to place Mitchell in command of East Florida. Mitchell was allowed to keep troops in Florida while creating his own state militia.

In 1812, Mitchell mobilized a detachment of his state militia in an attack against Florida and initiated the Florida Patriot War. In response, Spanish authorities again utilized Black military service to protect themselves. The garrison at St. Augustine consisted of 400 Whites and 500 Blacks. It is important to note the fact that not all of the runaways joined the Seminoles or Black Seminoles. There were those who placed themselves under Spanish rule. Black Seminoles, however, were in the most favorable position, as they lived in more strategic locations and were better trained in arms. The Spanish authorities looked to them as their most reliable allies in Florida.

In July of the same year, Mitchell voiced his complaints concerning the arming of Blacks by Spanish authorities, as well as the arrival of Black troops from Cuba. He was convinced that these measures would entice American slaves to revolt.

In late July, a Black man traveling throughout Florida warned both Seminole and Black Seminole villages that an attack was underway and that Whites planned to take their land and subdue them. On July 25, 200 Indian warriors and 40 Blacks from the Alachua region attacked the plantations along the St. Johns River, causing panic and desertion among the Georgia militia. By the end of the month, Mitchell's assumptions had proven correct. Slaves deserted plantations throughout the region, as well as in Georgia and South Carolina, to join the Indian and Black warriors. On July 30, US Col. Thomas A Smith reported "several hundred fugitive slaves from the Carolinas & Georgia [are] at present in their [Seminole] Towns & unless they are checked soon they will be so strengthened by [other] desertions from Georgia & Florida."

In order to prevent the influx of Black troops and supplies into St. Augustine, the United States instituted a blockade on the upper peninsula of East Florida. Their aim was to destroy St. Augustine by first reducing the strength of the garrison by cutting off the supply line, followed by an assault on the garrison, thus rendering the city defeated. Those plans were thwarted on September 12 by a group of approximately 50 Blacks and a small number of Indians led by a free Black named Prince Witen. In an ambush directed at US supply wagons, Witen and his men shot and scalped a sergeant in front of the troops. The rest of the troops were fired upon at point-blank range. Those who survived scattered, leaving the supply wagons behind. As a result, the American supply line was cut.

Blacks continued to fight throughout Florida, whether on their own initiative or under the command of the Seminoles or Spanish. For example, in Alachua, Blacks participated in the retaliatory battle against the United States for the ambush. The United States aimed its efforts at destroying both Seminole and Black Seminole villages alike. Heavy Black participation throughout the colony only increased the fear of a massive slave revolt. Thus, in its efforts, the United States focused their attention not only on destroying Black Seminole villages but, according to Brig. Gen. Thomas Flournoy, "Every Negro found in arms be put to death without mercy." Many Black and Indian Seminoles were forced to flee their villages and reside in the swamps. They were cut off from supply lines and dispersed, leaving the Alachua region open to American settlers.

A year later, they would emerge from the swamps and migrate westward toward the Suwannee River. Although the Patriot War had subsided, primarily due to the withdrawal of United States troops and the lack of continued support from the government, a sharp division within the Creek Nation caused tensions in the territory once again. The United States had become less occupied with the situation in Florida. This was due to the fact that during the Patriot War, the United States declared war on England and thus the War of 1812 commenced.

The Creeks were divided into two factions: the Upper Creeks, who were concentrated primarily in present-day Alabama, and the Lower Creeks, who were primarily living along the Chattahoochee River on the Georgia–Florida border. A civil war erupted in which the militant Creeks, known as the Red Sticks, were in conflict with those Creeks who were more amenable to negotiations with the United States. The Upper Creeks had been less exposed to White influence than the Lower Creeks, therefore, the growth of plantation society was not as readily accepted by them. Utilizing ammunition from Spanish authorities in Pensacola, approximately 180 Mississippi territorial militia, their Seminole allies and the Red Sticks attacked US forces about 80 miles north of Pensacola on July 27, 1813. In August, the Red Sticks struck yet another blow at Fort Mims, just north of Mobile. There, they massacred almost all the occupants of the fort. Blacks quickly began to occupy the same positions among the Upper Creeks (Red Sticks) as they had among the Seminoles and participated in joint war activities. As a symbol of this unity, most of the slaves were spared by Indian warriors.

The massacre at Fort Mims enraged the United States. By the fall of 1813, Gen. Andrew Jackson had entered the region with 3,500 Tennessee volunteers and approximately 1,000 Georgia volunteers. In November, the Red Sticks encountered the Americans. Blacks' fear of re-enslavement caused them to fight again alongside the Red Sticks. Recent runaways also accompanied the Red Sticks as they fought through the month of December. On December 23, a battle ensued just outside of present-day Montgomery in which 21 Creeks and 13 Blacks lost their lives. On March 27, 1814, Jackson crushed the Red Sticks opposition at the Battle of Horseshoe Bend. The majority of the Creek warriors fled south into Florida. The Creek War was steadily heading towards the Seminoles.

In 1814, the British commissioned Lt. George Woodbine to recruit as many Creeks and Blacks as he could for service to the British Crown. Woodbine entered Florida in May and set up his operations in Prospect Bluff, 15 miles from the mouth of the Apalachicola River. Approximately one month later, Woodbine arrived in Pensacola to organize the Red Sticks, provide them with food and ammunition, and recruit more runaways for service. By late August, Brevet Maj. Edward Nicolls of the Royal Marines had joined Woodbine in Pensacola. As a symbol of a unified front, Nicolls hoisted the Spanish flag alongside the British flag and declared himself commander of the city. Nicolls was welcomed by the downtrodden Spanish who had long since become exasperated in the war with Americans.

In November, Jackson clashed with Nicolls and Woodbine in a furious fight over Pensacola. In five days, Jackson captured Pensacola, forcing Nicolls and Woodbine to evacuate. The Blacks who participated with the English fled with them, given that they were promised their freedom and land in the British West Indies in return for their military service. These Blacks included over 100 fugitive slaves from the region alone. The British sailed approximately 150 miles east of Pensacola along the Apalachicola River and set up a fort at Prospect Bluff. Here they utilized the fort for negotiations with the Seminoles, remnants of the Red Stick Creeks, and the region's runaway slaves.

The War of 1812 officially ended on December 24, 1814, with

the Treaty of Ghent. Nicolls remained at the fort for another six months. In that time, he continued to train approximately 3,000 Indians and 300 Blacks. Nicolls' relationship with Blacks began before he entered present-day Florida, as Blacks were identified with him in Mobile. Apparently, a close bond was formed. In the summer of 1815, he arranged a meeting in London in order to garner an agreement to make the Creek and Seminole Indians military partners. The agreement was never made. The remaining Creeks and Blacks stayed at Prospect Bluff after the British left with those agreeing to relocate to the West Indies. The British left behind artillery that included vast amounts of ammunition.

In time, the majority of the Indians left the fort to create their own villages in the area. The Blacks remained at the fort under the leadership of a Black named Garcon. The fort, which became known as the Negro Fort, prospered under the leadership of Garcon. Garcon himself was a runaway slave and a 30-year-old carpenter. Blacks built a village behind the fort which included fields reaching out into the countryside. It encouraged perhaps another 1,000 Blacks to settle in the surrounding area.

The fact that former slaves and free Blacks lived and prospered nearby unsettled the American planters in the region. Protests were made by Jackson, who by this time had been appointed southern division commander to Spanish authorities. In April 1816, Jackson issued the following as an ultimatum to the Governor of Spanish Florida:

> I am charged by my Government to make known to you that a Negro fort, erected during our late war with Britain…is now occupied by upwards of two hundred and fifty Negroes, many of whom have been enticed from the service of their masters, citizens of the United States; all of whom are well clothed and disciplined. Secret practices to inveigle Negroes from citizens of Georgia, as well as from the Cherokee and Creek nations of Indians, are still continued by this banditti and hostile Creeks. This…may endanger the peace of the nation and interrupt

the good understanding which so happily exists between our
governments... The principles of good faith which always insure
good neighborhood between nations, require the immediate
and prompt interference of the Spanish authority to destroy or
remove from our frontier this banditti, put an end to an evil of so
serious a nature, and return to our citizens and friendly Indians
inhabiting our territory those Negroes now in said fort... I reflect
that the conduct of this banditti is such as will not be tolerated by
our government, and if not put down by Spanish authority, will
compel us, in self-defense, to destroy them.

In response, Spanish authorities expressed a willingness to
suppress the Blacks but informed Jackson that they could not do
the job. Florida Governor Zúñiga sent the following reply:

It gives me pleasure to understand that, their king as your
excellency thinks with respect to the necessity of destroying
the Negroes, the fort at Apalachicola occupied by them was not
constructed by the orders of the Spanish government; and that
the Negroes, although in part belonging to inhabitants of this
province, and as rational beings, may be subjects of the king,
my master, are deemed by me insurgents or rebels against
the authority, not only of his Catholic Majesty, but also of the
proprietors for whose service they have withdrawn themselves;
some seduced by the English Col. Nicholls, Maj. Woodbine,
and their agents, and others from their inclination to run off.

This evidently was true to a certain extent. The Americans
were not the only ones interested in returning runaway slaves.
Spanish Governor Mauricio de Zúñiga was not able to send troops
to the fort. However, he did send Captain Vincente Pintado to
investigate and return runaway slaves belonging to Spanish owners.
With the assistance of the British, Pintado entered the Negro Fort
with a list of 136 runaways including Garcon himself. However,
British authorities would not allow Pintado to seize any Blacks
by force. British and Spanish authorities could not agree on the
conditions of freedom for the Blacks at the fort. Nicholls responded
that the Blacks at the fort had already obtained their freedom.

Captain Pintado interviewed 128 runaways and 28 agreed to return with him.

Frustrated by the reply of the governor and thoroughly convinced that this "black insurrection" was bolstered by the Spanish, Jackson ordered the destruction of the Negro Fort in 1816. Gen. Edmund P. Gaines was given the order to destroy the fort and return the Blacks to their owners. Gaines began by erecting Fort Scott just inside the Georgia border but clearly close enough to initiate responses by the Negro Fort. He commissioned two gunboats to carry supplies to the fort along the outskirts of the Apalachicola. Lt. Col. Duncan Clinch was in command and given the orders not to enter the Apalachicola but to travel in plain view along the junction of the Flint and Chattahoochee Rivers. It was Gaines' hope that the Negro Fort would act upon them and give him a reason to attack.

On July 17, the Negro Fort's defenders gave Gaines his wish when a gunboat was sent out to retrieve water. Blacks ambushed and killed almost the entire crew except for two survivors of whom one was captured. Gaines had waited for this opportunity. He immediately dispatched Clinch's command down the river toward the fort. Along the way, Clinch encountered a party of Lower Creeks on a slave-hunting mission. He immediately commissioned them, supplying them with powder, guns and a promise of clothes from the fort. He also guaranteed them a payment of $50 for each American slave captured. Clinch's fortunes continued to increase as they got closer to the fort. The Lower Creeks intercepted a messenger from the fort carrying a White man's scalp on his belt. The messenger had been sent to the Seminoles for help. Now Clinch swiftly advanced toward the Negro Fort knowing that reinforcements were not on the way.

As the United States force and its Lower Creek allies approached the fort, Blacks immediately fired their cannons. Clinch ordered the Blacks to surrender to which the Blacks only cheered after the second volley of cannons. Clinch ordered the gunboats up to the fort which immediately caused the Blacks living outside the fort to abandon their villages and disperse into the forest.

On the tenth day of the expedition, the American forces came within range of the Negro Fort. Cannon volley was exchanged. The shells of the American force were unable to penetrate the walls and the inexperience of the Blacks sent shells hurling overhead, doing more damage to the banks of the river than anything else. During the ninth round of volleys from the gunboats, the United States was able to strike a blow that would immediately destroy the fort. A shell that was heated red-hot landed in the main ammunition supply area of the fort causing a terrible explosion; out of the 374 Blacks in the fort, 270 were killed instantly. In the end there were approximately 50 survivors. Garcon and his Choctaw Indian counterpart were captured. The Choctaw was scalped and stabbed to death, while Garcon was shot. The remaining survivors were taken into custody and returned to slavery. Those Blacks who dispersed into the forest fled toward the Black and Seminole villages.

The destruction of the Negro Fort stunned Blacks living in the region as well as the Florida Territory. The Blacks who lived in close proximity to the fort and were affiliated with it began to reorganize themselves closer to Seminole villages. In essence, the destruction of the fort resulted in the increase of the Black Seminole population. These particular Blacks began to cohabitate with Black Seminoles and establish stronger bonds with Seminole Indians. Their villages now extended down the eastern coast as far as Tampa Bay. They also chose Bowlegs as their king and were placed under the Black Seminole leadership of Nero, Bowlegs' principal or chief slave. Under Nero's command, the Black Seminoles began organizing themselves in preparation for retaliation. They swore revenge and were anxious to fight.

Nero is the most prominent Black Seminole leader during the First Seminole War. Territorial conflicts and the unquenchable thirst of Americans for slaves kept East Florida on alert for attacks by either side. The expansion of the plantation system southward would continue to exacerbate the tensions between Seminoles and Whites. For Nero, there was no way to avoid a conflict as his village and other Black Seminole villages under his command were geographically situated in the path of the plantation system's southward movement.

In the fall of 1817, Gen. Gaines erected a United States fort directly across the Flint River from a Seminole village then known as Fowl Town. Gaines ordered his men to cross the river in search of timber. Chief Neamathla of Fowl Town informed Gaines that his men had come onto Seminole land to cut timber and that it was a trespass that was not to be tolerated. Gaines informed Chief Neamathla that the land in question was part of the American soil granted in a treaty with the Creek Nation. Furthermore, Neamathla was now subject to US laws. Chief Neamathla replied that the Creeks had no right to cede any Seminole land to them and that the treaty did not mean anything to them. Earlier, he had warned Maj. David Twiggs, "Not to cross or cut a stick of wood on the east side of Flint River."

When Gaines called for Neamathla to attend a meeting, the latter declined due to lingering distrust. Gaines ordered Twiggs along with 250 soldiers to bring Neamathla to the fort for a meeting. The Seminoles resisted by firing upon the troops. The United States returned fire, causing the Seminoles to flee. A larger contingent of soldiers returned two days later under Lt. Mathew Arbuckle. Neamathla did not adhere to the demand for a meeting. The two forces exchanged gunfire yet again. This time, when the Seminoles fled the village, the United States troops, unable to capture Neamathla, burned the village to the ground The Seminoles wasted little time before they responded to the attack. Less than two weeks later, they ambushed a United States military boat traveling up the Apalachicola River killing nearly all aboard. A few days later they trapped a fleet of five US vessels for four days. Two officers were killed and 13 were wounded. Troops from the nearby Fort Scott rescued the fleet. Black Seminoles participated in both attacks.

For Nero, his leadership would soon be tested and proved in both diplomacy and battle. In December, warriors from Fowl Town captured two White agents of a British trading firm and tried them for their alleged participation in the Negro Fort destruction. Nero intervened on the White men's behalf and sent them into protective custody under the Spanish command. His intervention demonstrated the Black Seminoles' authority and respect among the Seminoles.

Nero was unaware of the furious offense that Americans had taken over the massacre of the first military boat. Andrew Jackson returned to the region as the new commander in Florida replacing Gen. Gaines. He entered East Florida with a zeal for revenge. Women and children had died aboard the ship, and America was outraged. He quickly moved up the Apalachicola River, sacking Seminole villages along the way. Nero was warned that Jackson was headed toward Chief Bowlegs' town, as well as the Black Seminole villages on the Suwannee. According to Alexander Arbuthnot, a Scottish trader and ally to Bowlegs, "the main drift of the Americans…is to destroy the black population of Swany."

Nero prepared for the attack by removing their women, children and cattle to the opposite side of the river where they would be safe. He quickly organized all the Black Seminole men from the villages in the area. The Black Seminoles had underestimated the size of Jackson's regiment. They were trapped on one side of the Suwannee, while Bowlegs and the larger contingent of Seminole warriors were on the other. Despite a valiant effort, the Black Seminoles, being greatly outnumbered, were forced to flee the area. It can be deduced that Nero was killed as there is no further mention of him in any of the records. While some historians view the Battle of the Suwannee as a defeat for the Black Seminoles, the Black Seminoles were quite successful in holding off the military forces long enough to allow their families to escape.

Shortly thereafter, Jackson crossed the Suwannee River and attacked Bowlegs' village. The Seminoles, along with the Black Seminole survivors, were defeated. They were forced to retreat into the nearby forest and swamps as Jackson burned the Seminole villages. The defeat of Bowlegs marked the end of the First Seminole War.

The destruction of the Negro Fort may also be viewed as the opening act of the First Seminole War. The question becomes: what makes the destruction of Fowl Town the first act of the war and not the destruction of the Negro Fort in the perspective of some historians? Evidence from previous battles indicates that had the messenger reached the Seminoles, they would in all likelihood have been involved in the battle. From the United States perspective, the issue of slavery, particularly the return of Black runaways, was one of the primary factors motivating the hostilities between the United States and the Seminoles. Andrew Jackson's military operations during the war indicate that both Seminole Blacks and Indians were considered a common foe.

In a letter, Jackson referred to the First Seminole War as a "savage and Negro war." Also, years later, John Prince, a Black resident in the Suwannee region under Nero's leadership, testified that Indians said "they would not have been attacked at the Suwannee, if they had not these Negroes—among them; that the [US] hope of getting possession of them invited the attack and proved the destruction of the town." Thus, the destruction of the Negro Fort was indeed the beginning of the First Seminole War. Furthermore, when historians assert that the attack on Fowl Town was the first act of the war, they are relegating the Black Seminoles simply to the role of Blacks in the company of Seminoles or Seminole slaves in the recordings of the Seminole Wars.

Andrew Jackson continued his military campaign into 1819

attacking Spanish forts and executing two of the remaining British occupants in Florida. By February, the Spanish were no longer able to maintain control over Florida. Thus, the Adams–Onis Treaty was signed between Spain and the United States ceding Florida to the United States for a price of five million dollars and the release of American claims to Texas. The formal transfer would not take place for another two years. In 1821, the Florida Territory formally became a United States possession. Although his tenure only lasted a few months, Andrew Jackson became the Provisional Governor. In July, Indian subagent Jean Penieres provided Jackson with a territorial review of the land and its inhabitants, including the following concerning Black Seminoles:

> We must add to this enumeration…fifty or sixty Negroes, or mulattos, who are maroons, or half slaves to the Indians. These Negroes appeared to me far more intelligent than those who are in absolute slavery; and they have great influence over the minds of the Indians. It will be difficult to form a prudent determination with respect to the maroon Negroes who live among the Indians on the other side of the little mountains of Latchiove. Their number is said to be upward of three hundred. They fear again being made slaves under the American government and will omit nothing to increase or keep alive mistrust among the Indians, whom they in fact govern. If it should become necessary to use force with them, it is to be feared that the Indians will take their part. It will, however, be necessary to remove from Florida this lawless group of free boaters, among whom runaway Negroes will always find refuge. It would perhaps be possible to have them received at St Domingo, or furnish them the means of withdrawing themselves from the United States.

Penieres' review reveals two very pertinent aspects of the future relationship between the United States and the Seminoles. The first is the recognition of the intricate relationship between Blacks and their Indian counterparts. The second is the introduction of the concept of Seminole removal from the territory.

For Black Seminoles, Florida's cession to the United States meant that they were down to their last and most trusted ally. They understand that their plight and fate was intricately tied to that of the Seminoles. Black Seminoles would begin to migrate in patterns directly parallel to their Seminole counterparts, constructing villages in close proximity and placing themselves under the protection of Seminole chiefs. Leadership changes among both groups witnessed a lateral shift for Black Seminoles within the Seminole Nation as a whole. Contact with Whites occurred more often as negotiations between Seminoles and the United States increased. Thus, Black and Indian codependency now extended even more into the area of diplomacy.

As stated earlier, Black Seminoles were afforded the autonomy to create their own communities outside of Seminole Indian villages. Within those communities, a hierarchal structure existed reflecting the one in Seminole Indian culture. There existed a Black Seminole chief who in most cases had established family ties or a close bond with Seminole Indian teachers in the adjoining village. Below the chiefs were sub-chiefs who directly assisted the chief in the management of the village and in his absence performed the duties thereof. Black Seminole leaders were held responsible for the upkeep and maintenance of the village. They were the final arbiters in all matters concerning the community. They were subject to the counseling of the elders in the community, especially when settling disputes.

Due to their familiarity with Whites and plantation society, Black Seminole leaders often served the Seminole Nation as advisers and interpreters between Indians and the US. Initially, Black Seminole leaders were considered sub-chiefs within the nation. However, as negotiations and interactions between Whites increased, they began to be recognized as chiefs. The recognition of the Black Seminole leaders as chiefs seems to indicate that the Seminole Indians recognized the autonomy of the Black Seminoles in general. The change in attitudes in essence reflects the existence of Black Seminoles as a nation within a nation. The mere fact that it would be years later before the United States officially recognized the Seminoles as a nation is irrelevant.

In 1821, the United States government immediately sought the solidification of their control over the Florida Territory. An early effort in this regard involved the signing of the 1826 Treaty of Indian Springs. This treaty was basically an agreement on the terms of all claims, debts and properties in question between the United States and the Creek Nation. The properties in question included land but particularly the ownership of runaway slaves. This treaty was signed under the influence of the same ideals that led to the attack on Fowl Town. Both Creeks and Americans still viewed the Seminoles as a part of the Creek Nation. Thus, any agreement with the Creeks was equivalent to one with the Seminoles. However, for Creeks, it also further signified the division within the Creek Nation due to the fact that only the Lower Creeks (Andrew Jackson's allies) signed the treaty. For America, it provided the ability to remove the Black Seminole threat to plantation society, as well as return slaves to plantation slavery.

The treaty essentially eliminated virtually all claims by the Seminoles on the Black Seminoles, and made the Black Seminoles susceptible to slave-retrieval expeditions. Black Seminoles were now unilaterally placed under the control of America. Now, there was no question as to how the United States would deal with runaway slaves; it became a question as to exactly which Black Seminoles were in fact runaways.

In 1823, the disheartened Seminoles chose not to resist the Americans as they seized the last vestiges of Seminole land in the Alachua region. On September 18, Seminole leaders signed the Treaty of Moultrie Creek which ceded all claims in Florida except for a reservation located miles away and cut off from the sea. Included in this treaty was a promise by the Indians to allow

Americans to apprehend runaway slaves. According to Article 7 of the treaty:

> The chiefs and warriors aforesaid…stipulate to be active and vigilant in the preventing the retreating to, or passing through, the district of country assigned them, of any absconding slaves, or fugitives from justice; and deliver the same to agent, who shall receive orders to compensate them agreeably to the trouble and expense incurred.

Evidence reveals that Seminoles had no intention of completely honoring this portion of the treaty as several groups of Black Seminoles were not listed, including the primary Black Seminole community, Peliklakaha. The Moultrie Creek Treaty was flawed and destined to fail from its inception. The land designated for the reservation was difficult for Seminole Indians and Black Seminoles because of poor soil. Two years later, Florida Governor William DuVal would declare: "The best of the Indian lands are worth but little…[and] is by far the poorest and most miserable region I ever beheld." In South Florida, the Seminoles would also suffer a drought. In December 1825, Lt. Col. George Brooke reported, "The major part of their nation is…suffering…unless the government assists them, many of them must starve."

Other problems existed in that some Seminoles would adhere to relocation at their own pace. Both Black and Indian Seminoles were slow to leave the prosperous Alachua region and remained on the land until Whites began to inhabit the area. Also, for those who adhered to relocation, there existed a problem with the economic compensation to be provided the Seminoles. The government was slow to distribute the provisions guaranteed to the Seminoles. It became a device for giving Whites the upper hand in their relationship with Indians. For the Black Seminoles, it meant that their Seminole Indian counterparts were forced to return runaway slaves as a result of the threat of withholding provisions.

It would seem as though this would have caused a major division between Blacks and Indians. In fact, by 1826, it was reported that so many runaway slaves were returned that an estimate of less than 50 were still at large. This estimate did not include the approximately 800 Seminole slaves reported in 1822. However, it is important to remember that within the Black–Indian relationship, Seminoles would allow the return of runaways, but if those slaves absconded again, would allow their return. As a result, Blacks were becoming more and more self-reliant, as their leadership began to understand that they would ultimately always have a different relationship with the government from that of their Indian counterparts.

Black Seminole chiefs such as Abraham (who became the principle leader) began to understand that the survival of their people rested upon their ability to negotiate better terms for themselves. It could no longer be left up to their Indian counterparts as they themselves were forced into a struggle for their own survival. In order to achieve these better terms, Black Seminole leaders undertook the task of convincing their Indian counterparts that a unified front during negotiations must still be sought whenever possible. They also became more intricately involved in matters within the Seminole Nation. What occurred during the 1820s was the further development of both Black Seminole leadership and Black Seminoles as a nation within the Seminole Nation. Black Seminoles had established themselves through cultural exchange, agricultural contributions, and military involvement, and now involved themselves in the political process, both internally and externally.

The relationship between Black Seminoles and Whites continually deteriorated throughout this period. Much of the blame for the continued flow of runaways was directed towards the Seminoles. In DuVal's 1826 letter to the Seminoles (mentioned in Chapter II), he warns them that Blacks, especially the runaways, were a detriment to their society. He counseled them as such:

> You are not to mind what the Negroes say; they will lie, and
> lead you astray, in the hope to escape from their white owners,
> and that you will give them refuge and hide them. Do your
> duty and give them up. They care nothing for you, further than
> to make use of you, to keep out of the hands of their Masters.

DuVal's letter was apparently part of a ploy by Whites to separate the Seminole Nation. For example, in the same letter DuVal further states:

> Thus far the negroes have made you their tools, and gained
> a protection, contrary to both justice and the treaty, and, at
> the same time, laugh at you for being deceived by them. Your
> conduct in this matter is cause of loud, constant, and just
> complaint on the part of the white people. Deliver them up, rid
> your nation of a serious pest, and do what, as honest men, you
> should do; then your white brothers will say you have done
> them justice, like honest, good men.

It therefore became imperative for Black Seminole leaders to maintain not only a unified front, but also an authoritative position within the Seminole Nation in order to maintain a political climate that would suit the needs of their people. Their authority was most recognizable in their counseling and interpretations during negotiations with Whites, particularly during those negotiations concerning runaways. Governor DuVal noted that Blacks were "much more hostile to the white people than their Masters." He went on to claim that they were "constantly counteracting" his counsel to the Indians and that there were instances where the Indians had agreed initially but reneged after talking with Black Seminole leaders.

The Seminole removal policy, which officially began in 1830, represented irreparable damage to the Seminole Nation. For the Seminole Indians, it would destroy the clan and kinship structure of their society. The father would own land and become head of the family. The matrilineal distinctions of kinship ties would become far less significant. The clan would be weakened through the loss of its basic economic and political functions. For Black Seminoles, the marginalization of Creek and Seminole Indians out west would place them in an unacceptable position of slavery among the Creeks, provided they emigrated along with the Seminole Indians.

In 1832, Col. James Gadsden, under the instruction of Secretary of War Lewis Cass, met with Seminole leaders, at Payne's Landing on the Ocklawaha River, to obtain an emigration agreement. Those instructions included a promise of annuities to be paid through the Creeks. This indicates that as late as 1832, the Seminoles were still not recognized as a nation but instead a part of the Creek Confederacy. Once again, the government, looking for the upper hand, utilized the devastating effect of the previous year's drought on the Seminole harvest to its advantage. Gadsden offered food as an incentive for removal. Black Seminole leaders Abraham and Cudjo were present. Cudjo was present as an agent for the US military. By 1834, he would be designated as a "regular interpreter at the Seminole agency."

The most arduous task for Gadsden in the negotiations was convincing the Seminole Indians to combine with the Creeks and settling the claims of slaves within the Seminole Nation. When dealing with the issue of claims, Gadsden remarked that "Many claims are for Negroes…The Indians allege that the depredations were mutual, that they suffered in the same degree, and that most of the property [slaves] claimed was taken as reprisal for property of equal value lost by them."

On May 9, 1832, the Treaty of Payne's Landing was signed. It gave the Seminoles approximately five million acres of land in the Arkansas Territory. It also provided the Seminoles with a settlement of $3,000 a year for 15 years, in addition to a one-time payment of $15,400 for Florida lands improved by the Seminoles. The Seminoles agreed to pay $7,000 to the United States for compensation of claims made against those Black Seminole members considered runaways. It is important to remember that Whites made a distinction between

Seminole slaves or Black Seminoles and runaway slaves. For Black Seminoles, the $7,000 payment suggested that their families as well as their communities would be kept intact. The treaty was still contingent upon the satisfaction of the Seminoles with the land in the Arkansas Territory.

In the winter of 1832–1833, a delegation that consisted of seven Seminole Indians, Indian agent John Phagan, Abraham and Cudjo traveled to the Arkansas Territory to inspect the land. At Fort Gibson on the Arkansas River, the second part to the Payne's Landing Treaty was signed. The Treaty of Fort Gibson basically stated that the Seminoles were satisfied with the land granted to them in the Arkansas Territory, and that they agreed to live within the Creek Nation but in a separate area, nevertheless becoming a part of the Creek Nation.

Immediately upon the delegation's return to Florida, the Seminole Nation abruptly refused to accept the treaty. There were several problems with the Fort Gibson Treaty. The first issue the Seminoles raised was the fact that the delegation had no authority to sign the treaty. Chief Micanopy told Indian agent Wiley Thompson that after their council with the Seminole delegation they decided to decline the offer. There is a version of events that states that Phagan forced the delegation to sign by threatening to refuse to guide them home. Four of the seven Indians later stated that they never signed the treaty. Thompson replied to Micanopy that the delegation had signed; therefore, he was to prepare his people for emigration. Abraham returned to Thompson with this reply: "The old man says today the same he said yesterday, the nation decided in council to decline the offer."

The treaties of Payne's Landing and Fort Gibson ultimately proved to be a serious threat to the Black Seminoles' freedom. Although the Seminoles were to pay $7,000 for Blacks, the placing of the Seminole Indians within the Creek Nation ultimately would leave Black Seminoles unprotected by their Indian counterparts.

The threat of the loss of protection was continuously bolstered by the persistent acts of kidnapping by the Creeks. Military authorities and government officials continued to separate Blacks and Indians politically, as well as physically. Therefore, Black Seminoles began to view the Creek–United States alliance as a major threat once again. The physical separation also provided Creek kidnappers with greater opportunities.

Thus, the Creeks' persistent pursuit of ownership and control of Black Seminoles further complicated the removal of the Seminoles for all involved. For the Seminole Indians, it represented two concerns that caused even those Indians who initially favored emigration to now object to a removal that would unite them with Creeks. The primary concern was the loss of Black Seminoles. For Black Seminoles, emigration to the West under the Fort Gibson Treaty guaranteed their enslavement. According to Potter, the Creeks' initiative to incorporate Seminoles into their nation was "evidently with a view to dispossess the Seminoles, in the easiest manner, of their large Negro property."

The second major concern was a fear that Creeks would extend no justice to them once they were outside of the United States' jurisdiction. Without a separate Indian agent to address their concerns, Seminoles feared being engulfed by the larger Creek Nation and exterminated as a culture. Their loss would not stop at the Black Seminoles. Seminoles argued that the Payne's Landing Treaty which guaranteed their property (particularly Seminole "slaves") could not be assured once they were in the West. Indian agent Thompson, when dealing with the property rights of Seminole slaves, agreed, reporting, "As it would be difficult, not to say impossible, to prove that negroes claimed by the Creeks, now in the possession of the Seminole Indians, are the identical Negroes, or their descendants...I cannot conceive that the Creeks can be supposed to have a fair claim to them." The loss of the Black Seminoles to the Seminole Indians would represent the beginning of their extermination.

The Creek–United States agreement, through various treaties, began with Creek claims on Black Seminoles. The essence of the Creeks' position with the United States in relation to Black Seminoles was that they had been kidnapping their own property. The annuities for slave property had been covered in pre-existing treaties for removal. Therefore, the Creek Nation began to demand the return of what they saw as their slaves. For the United States, this would ultimately mean that White lives, time, money and effort would have been wasted if they were to honor the Creek agreement and turn the Black Seminoles over to the Creeks for an emigration trip westward.

The United States, which further evidence will demonstrate, had no intention of allowing runaways to leave Florida. It would serve no purpose to separate them from their Indian counterparts, wherever this counterpart might go. It is important to understand that the government continuously maintained a respect for property rights. Therefore, the government made the distinction between runaway slaves and Seminole slaves within the Black Seminole population. This was, however, not the case with Whites in Florida. The constant pressure from Whites on the government to garner as many Blacks as possible for their plantation regime would dictate the policies concerning the Seminole Nation.

In 1834, Thompson would conditionally try to convince the Seminoles to emigrate peacefully. His constant offers of assurance that the Seminoles' property would be protected from the Creeks would fall mostly on deaf ears. As far as Micanopy was concerned, the Moultrie Creek Treaty did not expire for another nine years. This was the only treaty that concerned the Seminoles. The Payne's Landing and Fort Gibson treaties to Micanopy were nonexistent. The mood of the Seminoles was changing. Complete distrust of Whites became the primary sentiment as younger leadership began to arise among the Seminole Indians. Of these new leaders, one in particular would go on to become the government's most formidable foe. During a meeting on October 23, 1834, between Thompson and various Seminoles, the young leader named Osceola disrupted the conference by plunging his knife through a document on Thompson's table and declaring, "The only treaty I will ever execute will be this!"

Osceola's life began in the Creek Nation of Alabama. His mother at the time of his birth was married to a White man named Powell. There is no evidence that Powell was his biological father, yet he became commonly referred to by Whites as Powell. It is known that his heritage included the White race; a Scotsman and Red Sticks leader known as Peter McQueen proved to be his uncle. He was never accepted by Whites; in fact, he was belittled and reviled by Whites as a youth until he was driven out of Alabama. During the First Seminole War, he was captured but ultimately either escaped or was released. He shortly settled among the Tallahassee Tustenuggees and became known as such.

He is described as having piercing eyes and chiseled lips. Thompson recalled him to be "bold and dashing." It seems as though Osceola was generally a mannerly man, but was easily irritated during negotiations and unapologetic for the change in his mannerisms. In time, Osceola would rise in rank to a war leader, becoming a serious concern for Whites. As he ascended within the Seminole Indian community, his relationship with Black Seminole leaders would strengthen. He would ultimately become one of the Black Seminoles' most trusted allies during the Second Seminole War.

In April 1835, Thompson would make his last attempt at negotiating with the Seminoles. Here again, Osceola would end any successful agreement by declaring, "I will make the white man red with blood; and then blacken him in the sun and rain, where the wolf shall smell his bones and buzzards liven upon his flesh." Conflict was now inevitable. Shortly thereafter, Thompson would arrest Osceola for his repeated insults and threats. After six days of confinement, Osceola agreed to emigration. Thompson, in either his naiveté or overconfidence in the authority of Whites, presented Osceola with a rifle for his cooperation and believed that Osceola was no longer a threat to Seminole removal.

The government then declared that on January 8, 1836, all Seminoles must be in Tampa Bay and begin their emigration westward. In this declaration, they also issued a warning that if not, the United States Army would hunt them down. Black Seminoles were now face to face with the harsh reality of re-enslavement. The persistent conflict over slave ownership between Indians and Whites meant that any common Black Seminole could be either kidnapped or claimed by Whites and placed in slavery. Skirmishes between the Seminole Nation and the US government during the summer of 1835 were preludes to war. Black Seminole warriors from Minatti under the leadership of (Black Seminole) Harry were heavily involved. Around that time, Osceola issued a warning to any Seminole chief that conceded to emigration.

In November, Chief Charley Emathla was executed by Osceola, Holata Mico and Abraham for compliance with emigration. Emathla had sold his cattle and become an agent for the military, convincing other chiefs to do the same. Abraham protested the murder but Osceola scattered the gold over the chief's body stating emphatically, "See, it is the price of your blood." Other chiefs who had also agreed to emigrate quickly rushed to Tampa Bay after Osceola's warning. One chief in particular, Chief Econohatomico (also known as Red Ground Chief) reached Tampa Bay on November 14. Only days after, White slavers raided his settlement, seized a number of Black Seminoles and reduced them to slavery in Georgia. The chief's Black granddaughter was among the captives. To the rest of the Seminoles (both Indian and Black), this was the proof they needed to confirm the treachery of the Whites.

In December, the skirmishes would escalate to planned attacks on plantations in the Alachua and St. Johns River regions. On December 17, Black and Indian Seminoles raided plantations in the Alachua region. Ten days later, raids were executed in the St. Johns River region. These raids would continue throughout January. The plantation raids were carried out with two objectives in mind. The first was to strike a blow at plantation society in order to have Whites suffer the hardships of losing their homes and property, much like the Seminoles endured during the destruction of their villages. The second goal was to garner supplies and entice slaves to join their cause. The second objective heavily involved the Black Seminoles. Abraham was responsible for the strategic planning. As a result, two more Black Seminole leaders, John Caesar and John Cavallo, would attract the attention of the military as well as Whites in Florida's plantation society. Like Abraham, both men will be examined further in this study. The success of the plantation raids is implied by the fact that a majority of White settlers panicked and moved to either St. Augustine or Jacksonville for safety, leaving the frontier open once again for the Seminole Nation.

During the last week of December, Maj. Frances L. Dade and over 100 troops set out from Fort Brooke (at Tampa Bay) to Fort King (near present-day Ocala). At Fort King, they were to assemble with other units and execute Thompson's threat to hunt Seminoles down and round them up. The troops were being guided by a mulatto named Luis Pacheco, who was hired by the army for $25 a month for access to his knowledge of the area and Indian languages.

At the time, Louis Pacheco was a slave of a Spanish trader in the region. He was born on a plantation of Francis P. Fatio in the St. Johns River region. He was approximately 35 years old in 1835, which places his birth during the height of Seminole trading activity in the region. Between the frequent contact with traders and older siblings (a brother and sister) living with Indians, he was able to learn the Indian language. In 1824, he absconded from his abusive master and began living with Indians. As fate would have it, he was taken into custody and returned to servitude under Col. Brooke. He was transferred to other officers over a period of time until he was sold to Antonio Pacheco.

On December 28, 1835, Pacheco led Dade, along with his soldiers, through a piney area full of tall grass and palmettos approximately three miles from the Withlacoochee River and one mile south of the turn-off that led to Peliklakaha. One hundred and eighty warriors, both Indian and Black, arose from the tall grass and opened fire on the troops. Maj. Dade was killed instantly. Pacheco, who was right next to Dade, fell from his horse. Later, Pacheco would recall, "I immediately threw down my gun and lay down behind a tree, very much frightened...As I could speak the Seminole language, I begged each one for my life as they leveled their guns at me." As the fight ensued, Pacheco found himself in the middle of the battle. Pacheco contends that his life was spared on the orders of Sub-chief Jumper. He was then taken to a Black Seminole village where he states "the negroes made me feel quite at home," while the Indians "told me often that I would not live long if I misbehaved." By the end of the attack, there were only two soldiers still alive.

Pacheco's account of the attack, which became known as the Dade Massacre, has been challenged and has become a point of controversy regarding the Second Seminole War. Pacheco continuously maintained throughout his life that he knew nothing of the attack. He would later state that because of his luck, the Indians believed he used magic to make himself invisible. However, Whites believed he led Dade purposely into an ambush, while yet others believed he conspired with the Seminoles. Pacheco's short stint among the Seminoles did establish a relationship with the Seminole Nation. His siblings living within the Seminole Nation could certainly have fostered feelings of empathy and connectedness. Pacheco would also admit later in life that he was resentful of Dade for sending him out in the swamps and wilderness by himself to look for signs of hostilities. These three facts certainly bolster Coe's assertion that Pacheco may have met with the Seminoles and confided in them. Whether Pacheco was being truthful may never be known. What is known is that in 1838, he emigrated west with other Black Seminoles.

Blacks had open lines of communication in the region with Seminoles. According to Maj. F. S. Belton's account, "a Negro [Black Seminole leader]…named Harry, controls the Pea Creek band of about a hundred warriors, forty miles southeast of [Fort Brooke], who keeps this post constantly observed, and communicates with the Mick-asukians at Withlacoochee." Black Seminoles were also highly-active participants during the Dade Massacre. According to one of the two survivors, Private Ransom Clarke, the Black Seminoles were "more savage than the Seminoles." Clarke himself was shot in the shoulder by a Black Seminole "who, when he fired, cried out, 'There damn you!'" Clarke would also go on to state that he heard Blacks boasting and congratulating themselves for killing Whites or leaving them to die slowly. Seminole Chief Alligator later recalled, "When I got inside the log pen, there were three white men alive, whom the Negroes put to death after a conversation in English." Although what was said in this particular conversation is not known, he recalled Blacks ranting, "What have you got to sell?" which was a common question to Black Seminoles by soldiers when they visited the military posts.

Three days later, Osceola and Alligator led a band of 250 warriors into battle against United States forces under the command of Gen. Duncan L. Clinch. The Seminoles attacked the unsuspecting troops, who were unaware of the Dade Massacre, on the Withlacoochee River as they were attempting to cross. The battle became known as the First Battle of the Withlacoochee River or Clinch's Battle. During the battle, Osceola was shot in the arm. The wound, however, did not discourage him or his troops. By the end of the battle, four US soldiers died, while 59 were wounded.

The US troops were forced to retreat to Fort Drane. The Seminoles suffered three deaths, of which two were Black Seminoles, and five wounded. One month later, Osceola would write to Clinch, stating, "You have guns and so have we…you have powder and lead, and so have we…your men will fight and so will ours, till the last drop of the Seminole's blood has moistened the dust of his hunting ground." The Seminoles would go on to gain control of the Withlacoochee region. The Second Seminole War had officially begun.

On February 29, a combination of both Black and Indian warriors crossed the Withlacoochee River and headed towards Camp Izard. At Camp Izard, Gen. Gaines was building a post that would be a central point of departure for expeditions. Realizing that both their numbers and ammunition were too low for an assault, the warriors concealed themselves in the hummocks to the rear of the camp and waited for an opportune moment. The Seminoles knew that it would be virtually impossible to duplicate another Dade massacre. Their goals were to inflict enough damage to cause a withdrawal before reinforcements from Fort Drane (approximately 30 miles away) could arrive.

The bugle sounded reveille and for the soldiers the day would begin as normal. As the men proceeded from breakfast to their post, the warriors watched in silence. Approximately one-third of the men remained on duty at the half-completed post, while the rest worked on the riverbank chopping logs. There were only a few soldiers utilized as lookouts on the shoreline. They were totally unaware that the Seminoles had already crossed the river and were positioned on their flanks and to the rear. The warriors patiently waited until mid-morning before advancing.

Without the slightest hint of forewarning, Seminole battle cries accompanied a rifle assault. Unlike the panicked response of the soldiers during the Dade Massacre, soldiers dropped their axes and immediately reached for their rifles. Gen. Gaines himself was shot as warriors rushed in from behind a wall of smoke. He was struck in the lower lip resulting in the loss of two teeth. Seemingly unshaken by the attack or being shot, he was reported as saying, "It is mean of the redskins to knock out my teeth when I have so few!" The battle lasted for two hours. The Seminoles, satisfied with their attack, quickly retreated back into the hummocks. The warriors suffered but one casualty, while the soldiers suffered the same in death and 33 wounded. Gaines regrouped his soldiers immediately, ordered the completion of the camp and sent a runner to Fort Drane for immediate reinforcements and provisions.

The following afternoon, the warriors attacked Camp Izard again. This time, instead of a close-quarter assault, the warriors shot every soldier who was either by the riverbanks or exposed in the camp and visible from the hummocks. This assault would last for three days, resulting in much loss of life for the soldiers, and would be quite successful in lowering their morale and increasing their isolation. By early March, supplies for the camp were such that horses and dogs were eaten for meat. According to Lt. Prince, "A quarter of dog meat sold for $5." Gaines' expedition to hunt Seminoles was quickly turning into a complete disaster.

Two days later, Black Seminole leader John Caesar went to Camp Izard and called for a parley. Capt. E. A. Hitchcock met with the Seminole delegation which was lead by Osceola. Seminole chiefs Jumper, Alligator and Holatta Mico made up the delegation for the Seminoles, while Abraham and John Caesar interpreted. Chief Jumper acted as the spokesman, while Abraham interpreted. The Seminoles called for a truce that would include the United States soldiers retreating from the Withlacoochee region and leaving them to live in peace. Gen. Gaines responded three days later, asserting that if the warriors withdrew from the region and participated in treaty negotiations, the United States military would cease attacking them. The Seminoles agreed that the Withlacoochee would mark the boundary between them.

However, before the negotiations could be completed, Gen.

Clinch's reinforcements from Fort Drane arrived. Upon immediate sight of the warriors, the soldiers fired upon the Seminoles, sending them retreating into the hummocks. The soldiers were unaware of the parley and disturbed what might have been the negotiations to end the war. On March 10, the famished soldiers returned to Fort Drane. Gen. Gaines would leave Florida shortly afterwards, claiming the Seminoles were "met, beaten, and, forced to sue for peace." The truth of the matter was that although the Seminoles' siege on Camp Izard was lifted, they still held the region.

Gen. Winfield Scott, who was appointed in January to lead the Florida campaign, ordered three divisions to move on the Seminoles from the north from Tampa Bay under Col. William Lindsay, south then west from the St. Johns River region under Maj. Reynold M Kirby, and from the southwest under Gen. Clinch. Scott's plan was to surround the Seminoles in the Withlacoochee region and advance a coordinated attack, hopefully crushing the Seminole opposition. Their movements would be coordinated by firing signal guns daily. Once they arrived at their designated positions, a cannon shot would be fired. The number of United States troops involved was approximately 4,800 men.

During this operation, the military was engaged in several battles with Seminole warriors as they passed through various regions en route to Withlacoochee. For example, on March 17, US soldiers were ambushed on the east bank of the St. Johns River. On March 30, approximately 50 warriors attacked troops in the Alachua region near Peliklakaha. The next day, troops entered the abandoned Peliklakaha and burned it down. Unable to actively engage the Seminoles, Scott was replaced by Governor Call in May. For the next five months, these examples would be characteristic of the war, until October, when direct confrontation was no longer avoidable.

On October 1, warriors informed the Seminoles that troops were rapidly advancing upon them. Knowing that they were greatly outnumbered, the Seminoles were left with no choice but to take refuge in the Cove of the Withlacoochee. On October 12, five downtrodden warriors entered the new Seminole camp and informed them they had been attacked by troops and prisoners had been taken. Under pressure from the troops, a Black Seminole woman who had been captured divulged information as to the whereabouts of both Black and Indian villages in the region. This was the breakthrough the troops were waiting for. Up until this point, they were unable to openly engage the Seminoles and were primarily victims of various ambushes. As the troops advanced, Black and Indian warriors openly attacked troops in various places in the region. These engagements continued for the rest of the month.

The engagement on October 12 became known as the Second Battle of Withlacoochee or Call's Battle. During the battle, the Blacks and Indians developed a plan that involved strategic maneuvers from bands that were separated by the villages. The respect for each other as warriors as well as a joint nation was displayed often throughout the month. For example, when warriors attacked the troops who had captured the prisoners, they spared the life of the Black Seminole woman believing that she had been forced to reveal their villages, but they immediately shot an Indian guide named Billy for willfully betraying his people. Once again, United States troops were repelled from the Withlacoochee region back to Fort Drane; however, they would not go back to accept defeat. They would only go back in order to regroup.

In November, Governor Call returned to the Withlacoochee region with troops, Tennessee volunteers and approximately 750 Creek volunteers. Their numbers represented roughly half the amount originally sent by Scott earlier that year. Many of the volunteers from Alabama, Georgia and Tennessee had grown weary of the expedition and had returned home. On November 13, Call's troops crossed the Withlacoochee River and torched three large

Seminole villages. An elderly Black Seminole was taken prisoner as he was the only person encountered. He informed the troops that the rest of the Seminoles had relocated to the Wahoo Swamp. Call proceeded to the swamp with the Tennessee volunteers principally making up the right wing and the Creeks, the left. On November 17 and 18, the Seminoles would continue their tactic of ambush by assaulting the right wing. The engagement lasted approximately one hour and ended with a dispersal of the Seminoles, who were routed. For political reasons, the Seminoles chose to attack the right wing, preferring to fight the Whites instead of the Creeks.

The second engagement in the Wahoo Swamp was a major battle and the Seminoles suffered heavy losses. The United States troops estimated that at minimum 50 warriors were killed. The Seminoles were forced to retreat deeper into the swamp, so the troops pressed the attack, despite low provisions. On November 21, the Seminoles engaged the Tennessee militia again and quickly retreated further into the swamp. The militia pursued them into the swamp, regardless of the fact that they were "above their waists in mud and water" at times. The Seminoles were at their last stronghold. Their force totaled 620 men, of which approximately 200 were Black. As the Seminoles prepared for the final assault, the Creeks boldly dashed in through a shallow portion of the river but before the Creek leader could inform his warriors that the water was indeed shallow, he was shot down.

The Creek warriors returned fire without further advancement. The Seminoles were engaged with the Creeks for approximately one hour as the Tennessee militia tried to maneuver through the swamp. The troops arrived shortly after the volunteers finally made their way through, and it was they who noticed the shallow part of the river and commanded the militia to proceed with a bayonet charge. Unable to see the portion of the river that the commanding officer had informed them to pass through, the militia refused. This allowed the Seminoles time to hold off their pursuers. As night began to fall, the soldiers began to withdraw. Once again, the United States forces were unable to openly engage the Seminoles and defeat them. Governor Call had now failed twice to crush the Seminoles. As a result, he would be replaced in December by Gen. Thomas S. Jesup.

Thomas Sidney Jesup began his career in the military in 1808 as a commissioned second lieutenant of the Seventh Infantry. He first distinguished himself in the War of 1812. Afterward, he quickly rose through the ranks, becoming a brigadier general and quartermaster general of the army by 1818. Ten years later, he was promoted to major general. His first command against Indians would not be against the Seminoles. In May 1836, he was assigned to command US and Georgia troops in the Creek War.

On December 8, 1836, Jesup replaced Governor Call as commander of the army in Florida. His strategy was to utilize those tactics that were both orderly and most practical in routing the Seminoles and accomplishing the goal of submission as quickly as possible. He was careful to avoid making the mistake of underestimating the Seminoles and lacking an extensive knowledge of the Florida terrain as his predecessors did. Before he enacted any campaign, he wanted to determine the exact location and number of Seminoles in their strongest positions.

From Jesup's entrance into the Second Seminole War, he immediately recognized and understood both the military and political importance of the Black Seminoles. It therefore became a pertinent strategy to identify those strongholds that held a large number of Black warriors. Once Jesup determined that the Seminole strongholds were in close proximity, he decided to attack each separately in the hopes of isolating them. Instead of utilizing the approach of his predecessors, Jesup adopted the Seminoles' guerilla tactics. This strategy of utilizing their guerilla-style tactics was based on the premise that the military advantage of the Seminoles was their advanced knowledge of the Florida terrain, which included their ability to find food and shelter concurrent with their military movements.

Therefore, he developed a strategy that would utilize small groups of men to attack the Seminole villages. If he was able to destroy their food and shelter and dictate their movements to some degree, he felt that the Seminoles would be too concerned with survival to continue to hold off the troops. He went on further to create a regiment of Creek scouts to track Seminoles in order to gain a better understanding of their patterns of movement, as well as the strength of their warriors. He promised the Creeks the Seminoles' possessions, particularly their slaves. However, he would later rescind this promise.

Politically, the Black Seminoles were a delicate matter in negotiations with the Seminole Indians, as well as in the United States public arena. Both anti-slavery and pro-slavery activists kept a watchful eye on the war. Both sides used the Black Seminole cause as an argument for their stand on slavery. The longer the war lasted, the more the Black Seminoles became a central focus.

Jesup decided that if the Black Seminoles repudiated their opposition to emigration, then the Seminoles would comply with the terms of the Payne's Landing and Fort Gibson treaties. In all likelihood, this decision was based on the military's position that although in 1834 the Seminoles informed Indian agent W Thompson that they wished to be near their ancestors' graves, both Thompson and Secretary of War Lewis Cass believed that the fear of losing Blacks was the real reason for their refusal to emigrate. Furthermore, it was believed that the Seminoles' refusal to emigrate was indeed the idea of Blacks. However, the basic problem, which was the cornerstone of the conflicts leading up to and during the war, was determining which Blacks belonged to the Seminole Indians and which belonged to the White slave owners. Ultimately, the decisions that Jesup made in dealing with this issue dissatisfied both of the aforementioned, causing Jesup to fail in his efforts to end the war quickly.

Jesup's first decision was to locate Osceola. It was believed that he was still in the Wahoo Swamp region or had gone further south into the Everglades with Micanopy, Jumper and Abraham. In late December or early January, it was discovered that Osceola was still in the Withlacoochee region. He apparently was ill and had taken up residence in a Black Seminole village in the Panasoffkee Swamp. On January 10, 1837, United States troops, along with a few Creeks, surprised the Black Seminole village and captured 16 Blacks. Two days later, 36 more Blacks were captured including three belonging to Osceola's band.

Primus, a former slave, was one of the Blacks captured. United States troops were familiar with him as they had used him earlier as a messenger on at least two occasions. Primus was married to a Black Seminole, so the last time he left the company of Whites he never returned. After being threatened with hanging, Primus told troops that Osceola was in the swampy wilderness and that Chief Echo Emathla was still on the Withlacoochee River.

The army immediately marched down the river on both sides in search of both Osceola and Echo Emathla. On this expedition, they determined that the remaining Seminoles had fled the region, heading south through the swamp. To the military, this meant that Jesup's plans were to some extent yielding immediate results. Lt. Col. Foster was dispatched to scout for a camp of Seminoles just south of the mouth of the river. There, Foster's band encountered a group of Indian and Black Seminoles. The troops then took six Black Seminole men and 12 women and children into custody. Although Jesup was unable to find Osceola, he was content in the knowledge that the Withlacoochee region was for the most part free of Seminoles. He then continued to move south in search of Micanopy, Jumper and Alligator.

On January 22, 1837, the primary contingent of troops made its way south to the Ocklawaha River. There, a Black Seminole man was captured and most likely forced to reveal the whereabouts of the camp of Chief Osuchee (also known as Cooper), Micanopy's brother-in-law. Osuchee was noted for leading Black warriors at the Battle of Wahoo Swamp. In that battle, he had been shot and was now in the southern portion of Apopka Lake recuperating with a medicine man and other wounded, along with their families. The next day, the Creeks charged Osuchee's camp without orders and killed him. Cooper's wife and children, along with others, were captured, including two Black warriors and their families.

The captured prisoners informed the troops that the majority of Seminoles were headed in a southeast direction. Col. Archibald Henderson led a contingent of Alabama volunteers, United States mounted marines and Creek scouts after them. On January 27, they saw the Seminoles' herds of livestock grazing after spotting their trail. A band was immediately dispatched to locate the Seminoles. While collecting the cattle, the troops seized a Black Seminole who was in charge of guarding the cattle. He informed the troops that a large number of Black Seminoles, along with approximately 40 to 50 Indians under the command of Abraham, were nearby. Lieutenant James Chambers, who was in charge of another band dispatched to locate the Seminoles, discovered the Seminoles' baggage train. He captured five Indians,(two women and three children), approximately 20 Blacks (mostly women and children), and 100 ponies, of which half carried both possessions as well as supplies.

The remainder of the Seminoles around the baggage train escaped to the main body of Seminoles nearby. Major Morris, along with the Creek band, followed them immediately. In the Big Cypress Swamp, along the approximately 20-yard-wide Hatcheelustee Creek, Black and Seminole Indian warriors prepared for battle. They strategically placed themselves on the opposite side of their families to protect them while creating a cover for their escape. Just after noon, the warriors opened fire on the advancing troops.

Henderson's troops counterattacked, forcing the Seminoles to retreat further into the swamp and assume another defense.

Black Seminole families quickly dispersed deeper into the swamp. The warriors' position provided them with ample time and space to escape. However, one Black Seminole named Ben was captured, along with his wife, Jane, and infant son, Robert. Apparently, the family fell behind the other Blacks and subsequently stopped running as the troops commanded them to halt. Ben did not offer the troops any valuable military information, but instead stated that he had never been owned by a White man and that he belonged to Micanopy. The troops were unmoved by his plea and immediately took him and his family into custody.

Despite the fact that many Seminoles, particularly Black Seminoles, escaped the capture of their baggage train, Jesup claimed that the Battle of Hatcheelustee Creek was a tremendous victory. Jesup believed that the Seminoles would be prepared to discuss emigration again, now that they had suffered such a great loss of equipment, supplies and livestock. Jesup, however, was disappointed.

As it would turn out, Jesup was premature in his disappointment. Jesup soon discovered that Ben, one of the captured, was an influential character among the Black Seminoles. Jesup looked upon Ben as an interpreter whose former position of leadership would favorably impress the Seminoles. The fact that his family was also held prisoner assured Jesup that Ben could be trusted to relay his messages and return. On January 28, Ben left to locate Chief Jumper and tell him that Jesup wanted to negotiate. The general anxiously awaited his return.

When Ben arrived at the Seminole camp, he did not speak with Jumper, but with Abraham, his leader. He notified Abraham of the general's wishes to negotiate and gave him gifts from Jesup. One historical account is unclear as to why Ben would go directly to Abraham, but he did so because Abraham was his chief.

Furthermore, by going directly to Abraham, Ben's actions bolstered the case that the Black Seminoles in Florida were a nation within the Seminole Nation.

On January 31, Ben returned to Jesup with Abraham. Ben entered the camp first to advise them that Micanopy's leading Black Seminole was ready to meet. As Abraham entered the camp, soldiers muttered amongst themselves about the arrival of "the Nig[g]er who was going to hang." The exact content of their conversations is not known. However, it can be surmised that both parties agreed to listen to the other's wishes as Abraham agreed to bring in Jumper and Alligator for negotiations. Jesup now fully understood that in order for emigration to occur, he had to gain the assistance of the Black Seminoles. This assistance would not be acquired without extending considerations to them in the matter.

After some persuasion, Abraham convinced Jumper and Alligator to meet with Jesup. On February 3, the men agreed on a truce, along with the other principal chiefs who could be gathered together for negotiations. All agreed to meet Jesup at Fort Dade, located approximately 50 miles northeast of Tampa, on February 18. It is important to note that the negotiations for the Seminoles must have included other principal chiefs in the nation. Also, this truce did not include the entire Seminole Nation, as the Seminoles in the St. Johns River region continued their plantation raids throughout 1836 and into 1837. Black Seminole leader John Caesar would be the principal war chief until January 1837. He was simply unwilling "to do nothing" while the Seminoles in the Withlacoochee were being subdued.

Jesup appears to have been doubtful about the success of the upcoming negotiations. Although he looked forward to the treaty negotiations, he wrote, "I have required…immediate emigration; there would be no difficulty in making peace…were it not for that condition…The Negroes are all averse to removing to so cold a climate." Jesup readily acknowledged the importance of establishing a satisfactory agreement with the Black Seminoles. He also believed that an agreement with the Blacks could be separate from an agreement with the Indians. Jesup fully understood that he was not dealing with Blacks in the company of Seminoles or Seminole slaves, but a distinct group of people with power, influence and interests in the Seminole Nation. Thus, on March 4, when negotiations actually began, distinct proposals for Black Seminoles and Seminole Indians were discussed with each group's leaders.

The Seminoles would not begin to assemble at Fort Dade until February 19. Only Abraham arrived the day before to assure Jesup that the negotiations would take place. Approximately ten Black Seminoles were present during the negotiations. Black Seminoles were represented by Abraham; later during the negotiations, John Cavallo supposedly made his appearance. Negotiations began on February 24. However, when discussions came to a standstill, the Seminoles decided they could no longer negotiate as Micanopy was not present and talks had gone beyond their instructions. Micanopy wanted to remain in the swamps while Jesup insisted upon emigration. Representatives could not continue negotiations without Micanopy, therefore both sides agreed to continue talks on March 6. This would give Micanopy time to come. To ensure his arrival, Jesup kept 12 hostages, including a nephew of Micanopy.

On March 4, negotiations started again. Micanopy, for an undetermined reason, did not show, nor did Alligator. Both chiefs did, however, send men and authorized them to negotiate on their behalf. John Cavallo was one of the two men sent by Alligator to represent him. Two days later, an agreement titled The Capitulation of the Seminole Nation of Indians and their allies by Jumper, Holatoochee or Davy, and Yaholoochee, representing the principal chief Micanopy was signed. The "Articles of Capitulation," as it become commonly known, agreed that hostilities would cease immediately and permanently. The Seminoles agreed to assemble no later than April 10 for emigration.

For the Black Seminoles, Article V was the most important of the 11 articles that made up the capitulation agreement. It guaranteed the safe passage of Seminole Indians and their "allies and their Negroes" westward. Article V enraged the plantation owners. Pressure from this group would cause Jesup to rescind Article V by secretly negotiating an April 8 agreement with selective chiefs to return runaway slaves. In an effort to conceal this agreement, he ordered the separation of runaway slaves, which by this time numbered more than 700 Blacks.

Despite an effort to seize them without alarm, attempts to claim Blacks by White slave owners caused panic among the Black Seminoles who had assembled at various forts in expectation of emigration. Once the news spread, the Seminole Nation as a whole was then enraged. When Coa Hadjo announced in council that he had agreed to return fugitive slaves, Osceola furiously declared that as long as he was alive that would never happen. Osceola wholeheartedly agreed with the Black Seminoles. As Black Seminoles fled the forts, Seminole Indians began to refuse to assemble for emigration. Jesup ordered the capture of all Black Seminole leaders, but it was too late. In September, fighting began once again and the Second Seminole War was renewed.

By December 1837, the Seminole Nation was largely concentrated in South Florida in the Lake Okeechobee region. Black Seminoles were now reliant upon John Cavallo as their principal leader. Abraham had been held under strict supervision since his agreement to emigrate. Seminole Indians experienced a rift due to Coa Hadjo's secret agreement to return runaways. Osceola, the Seminole Indian chief whom they knew they could trust, had been captured. Their future was now in the balance. Some Black Seminoles grew weary of battle and began to turn themselves in to the troops. Col. Zachary Taylor, upon his recent arrival in Florida, proceeded southeast from Tampa Bay searching for Seminoles. On Christmas Day, the troops reached a swamp in the Okeechobee region. There, in a hummock just beyond this point, they would engage the Seminoles in battle.

In February 1838, a committee of Jesup's senior officers, headed by Brig. Gen. Abraham Eustis, implored Jesup to end the war by allowing the Seminoles to stay in South Florida. Jesup agreed and wrote to the president: "In regard to the Seminoles, we have committed the error of attempting to remove them when their lands were not required for agricultural purposes; when they were not in the way of the white inhabitants…My decided opinion is, that unless immediate emigration be abandoned, the war will continue for years to come, and at constantly accumulating expense." By March 7, approximately 300 Indians and 150 Blacks surrendered. A military surgeon described the Black Seminoles as "the most diabolical looking wretches I ever saw; their style of dress contributing much to render them ferocious and oriental in aspect."

Jesup was now thoroughly convinced that the key to ending the war was to settle the matter concerning Black Seminoles once and for all. Therefore, he issued an order stating "that all the Negroes [who were] the property of the Seminole…Indians in Florida…who separated themselves from the Indians and delivered themselves up to the commanding officer of the Troops, should be free…They should be sent to the west as a part of the Seminole Nation, and be settled in a separate village, under the protection of the United States." The declaration would appear to have accomplished the Black Seminoles' goals. However, the protection guaranteed by the troops seemed to only apply to those Seminole slaves. Therefore, the question of slave ownership was not completely answered. This would only increase the mistrust of Black Seminoles toward Whites. As a result, Jesup would spend the next two years convincing Black Seminoles of their safe departure out west. In an effort to do so, he would utilize Black Seminole leaders who had agreed to emigrate. In time, the principal Black Seminole chief, John Cavallo, would become one of those leaders.

To Jesup's dismay, his plan to allow the Seminoles to remain in Florida without their Black allies was rejected by the Secretary of War. Furthermore, he was ordered to continue with removal regardless of the present conditions. Jesup was now in a major dilemma. Hundreds of Seminole Indians had come in, believing that they were permitted to stay. He was now facing 513 Indians and 161 Blacks, of which 150 were warriors, assembled near Fort Jupiter. On March 21, he ordered their capture.

For Jesup, his order left him with feelings of dishonor. As far as the government was concerned, the capture was a great success, in that almost as many Seminoles (both Indian and Black) were seized as had either surrendered or been captured during the previous 15 months. Five principal Seminole Indian chiefs remained at large: Coacoochee (Wild Cat), Alligator, Sam Jones, Halleck Tustenuggee and Tiger Tail. Black Seminole leader John Cavallo was also still at large.

Jesup utilized persuasion to bring in Wild Cat, Alligator and John Cavallo. In March, Chief Holatoochee and Black Seminole leader Abraham accompanied Gen. Taylor to negotiate with Alligator. A pleased Taylor informed Jesup of Alligator, Cavallo and Coacoochee's pending surrender. He went on to report that "Alligator will send for Coacoochee [Wild Cat]." Jesup responded to the news: "If these three chiefs can be detached from the hostiles the war may yet be closed this summer." John Cavallo surrendered in mid-April. On April 25, Abraham wrote Jesup, stating. "All the black people are contented I hope…John Cavallo is in and contented." Although this was deemed as another major success, the war was still not over. In May, Jesup was replaced as commander by Gen. Taylor.

To Jesup's credit, Black Seminole leaders had surrendered and prepared for emigration. Jesup had successfully created a division between the Black and Indian Seminoles. The fact that Black Seminole leaders agreed to emigration demonstrates that although they were allies with the Indians, they maintained a separate goal during the war. This act by the Black Seminole leadership challenges the notions that completely submerge the Black Seminole experience within that of Seminole Indians.

For the remainder of the war, small numbers of Black Seminoles would continue to fight under the remaining Seminole Indian chiefs in Florida. They would no longer play significant roles in battle. They would participate in negotiations on the behalf of the Seminoles in the capacity of interpreter only. Black Seminole leaders, including Principal Chief John Cavallo and July (the second sub-chief of Peliklakaha), would continue to work with the government and convince Seminoles to emigrate until the war's end in 1842. For Black Seminoles, the last party of emigrants arrived in the West in 1841. Small numbers would remain in Florida, for the most part concealed in the dark hummocks and swamps below Lake Okeechobee. They would sporadically be involved in attacks on farms and plantations, primarily as a means to steal supplies.

The struggle for freedom would play an important role in the cultural development of Black Seminole society. The significance of their military service would allow them to increase their numbers, sustain their way of life and forge alliances with not only the Seminole Indians but also foreign powers as well. In time, their military experience would define Black Seminole society in a way that distinguished them from their Seminole Indian counterparts.

In the years following the Second Seminole War, Seminole Indians would begin to serve as slave catchers. There were two primary reasons for this. First, portions of the remaining Seminoles in Florida became somewhat subservient to the United States, causing them to cooperate whenever possible. More importantly, there were those Seminole Indians who became resentful towards their Black allies for utilizing their position between them and Whites to their own advantage. The fact that Black Seminole leaders eventually traded positions and supported the United States military left these particular Seminole Indians with a strong feeling of betrayal.

When examining the Black military experience as it relates to the development of the Seminole Nation and the Second Seminole War from their perspective, it causes historians to re-examine the war, while questioning the importance of Black Seminoles. The estimated numbers of participants reflects neither their importance in nor impact on the Second Seminole War. To continuously perpetuate the idea of docile Blacks in the company of dominating Indians is above all a misrepresentation of history. Black Seminoles developed a different objective from Seminole Indians during the war and for the most part accomplished it. As Seminole Indians fought to remain in Florida from 1838 to 1842, the majority of the Black Seminoles were securing their freedom by emigrating westward.

CHAPTER IV

BLACK SEMINOLE LEADERSHIP DURING THE SECOND SEMINOLE WAR

Black Seminole leaders utilized their trusted positions as interpreters and counsel to Seminole Indians to the advantage of their own community. While entrusted with positions of authority, they gained the ability to negotiate their own terms. Although agents of the United States government constantly objected to negotiating with former slaves, Black Seminole leaders were able to successfully engage them during negotiations. By examining the lives of three of the most prominent Black Seminole leaders during the Second Seminole War, this chapter will further examine Black Seminole involvement by demonstrating the autonomy of the leaders as well as the community itself. The most prominent leaders were: Abraham, John Caesar and John Cavallo.

Abraham

The most outstanding personality among the Black Seminoles was an illiterate runaway slave who, like many runaways in Florida, found peace among the Seminoles. However, unlike most Black Seminoles, this man's intelligence and influence was recognized by all. Abraham, referred to by Seminoles as Yobly, was also given the title "Prophet" by fellow Black Seminoles and "Sense bearer" by his Seminole comrades. Both his leadership and contributions to the Black Seminoles' quest for freedom in Florida rank Abraham with other great abolitionists, such as Samuel R. Ward, Henry Bibb and Mary Ann Shadd-Cary. There is no doubt that his accomplishments equal theirs. However, the difference between them is his lack of universal notoriety.

Generally, Abraham is believed to have been born between 1787 and 1791. One account places his birth in Georgia or another southeastern English-speaking state, while another account depicts him as born of slave parents (who were fugitives from Georgia) among the Seminoles in Pensacola. Given the known facts, it would seem most likely that parts of both accounts are accurate. Contradictory, somewhat proven, information makes it impossible to determine with absolute certainty whether he had any knowledge of the Spanish language. This raises questions as to the length of time spent in Pensacola. Also, as a young boy he was the slave of Dr. Sierra, a physician in Pensacola. This raises questions regarding the tale of a birth among Seminoles. It can be that he was born of slave parents from Georgia (not necessarily runaways) and raised as a slave of Dr. Sierra in Pensacola. All accounts of his years as a young boy in Pensacola do coincide. Abraham grew up within the city of Pensacola, suggesting that he most likely served as a domestic servant.

Descriptions of both Abraham's physique and mannerisms were often contradictory. The only consistency in these descriptions referred to the scar that appeared over his right eye. Based on the fact that these descriptions were primarily by American officers, it becomes obvious how the descriptions varied so wildly. For example, one officer describes Abraham as "a person erect and active, and in stature over six feet." Yet another describes him as "of ordinary stature, rather thin, with a slight inclination forward." The descriptions of his mannerisms and character were equally inconsistent. "Abraham is a non-committal man...with a countenance which no one can read" is one description that may best define him when negotiating with officers. It seems that his demeanor was directly related to the ulterior motives underlying negotiations and the circumstances surrounding any given meeting. "He always smiles and his words flow like oil," one person noted. "His conversation is soft and low, but very distinct, with a most genteel emphasis." He was also described as "plausible, pliant, and deceitful."

As a young boy, Abraham escaped a life of bondage with Dr. Sierra and fled to the Seminoles. In time, he became a slave to

Micanopy who later became a principal chief of the Seminoles. Abraham became a member of a Seminole community where he was afforded opportunities to develop as a leader. He would go on to gain the titles of interpreter, spokesman, sense bearer and chief counselor to Micanopy. He would also marry the widow of a former Seminole chief (as previously stated) and become the chief of Peliklakaha.

Peliklakaha's (also known as Abraham's Old Town) primary period of occupancy was from 1813 to 1836. During this period, Black Seminoles cultivated various foods such as beans, melons, pumpkins, corn, rice and other vegetables. Their livestock included horses, fowl and cattle. Peliklakaha, like all other Black Seminole towns, was a place of safety for its inhabitants. Black Seminoles maintained a peaceful coexistence with the Seminole Indians; however, they likely understood that their survival was predicated upon their strength in numbers and geographic contiguity. Their evolving sense of community fashioned a certain cultural autonomy which helped distinguish the group from their Indian neighbors. By 1826, there were over 100 Blacks residing in Peliklakaha. In 1836, Peliklakaha became a casualty of the Second Seminole War when the United States military dispersed the inhabitants by forcing them to flee and burned the town down leaving Peliklakaha in ruins.

Neither Abraham's military training nor conflicts with American soldiers began with the Second Seminole War. It is believed that in July 1814, Abraham was one of the Black slaves fighting alongside the British during the War of 1812, motivated by the promise of freedom and land in the British West Indies. The British force was in search of a base of support for an assault on New Orleans and recruited refugees from the Red Stick Creeks and runaway slaves from Pensacola. In November of that year, Gen. Andrew Jackson stormed Pensacola, forcing the British along with their Indian and Black allies (including Abraham) to flee the city. Abraham was then discovered at the Negro Fort (or Fort Negro). Exactly how he escaped the ill fate suffered by most Blacks when the fort was destroyed in 1816 is not known.

It, however, can be deduced that it was during this period in his life that he became directly affiliated with the Seminoles. Those Blacks who fought with the British aligned themselves with Chief Bowlegs on the Suwannee River. Chief Bowlegs was Micanopy's uncle. At that time, Abraham became somewhat of a protégé of both Bowlegs and Micanopy and resumed fighting against Andrew Jackson in 1818. In the battle of the Suwannee, Abraham gained both the recognition and trust typically reserved for Seminole warriors. As a result, he placed himself directly under the protection of Micanopy, who had now become Principal Chief of the Alachua.

Chief Micanopy was a direct descendant of one of the members of the original band of Alachua Seminoles. His authority was expanded when factions of the band settled in different areas of the region. Although the extent of his authority is not clear, it was understood that when he spoke all adhered. Gen. Clinch of the United States military described him as "a man of but little talent or energy of character, but from his age and wealth has much influence in the nation." He is physically described as approximately five feet, six inches, weighing around 250 pounds with a "fat, dull face set on a short neck".

Chief Micanopy was inclined to indulge himself on the privileges bestowed upon a man in his position. During the conflicts with Whites in the area which resulted in war, Micanopy was involved in the negotiations much more than in the actual fighting. This is not to say that he did not participate, but Chief Alligator was considered the war chief from the Alachua region, while Micanopy was considered non-aggressive. His position as head chief was considered more or less ceremonial. He was intelligent enough to surround himself with sensible and reliable counselors, who assisted him in delegating authority in some instances while manipulating him in others. Micanopy participated in all of the major negotiations until his capture and eventual emigration.

By the early 1820s, Abraham was Micanopy's interpreter. His first important role as an interpreter for Micanopy came during negotiations in Washington, DC, in 1826. Micanopy headed this delegation of Seminole chiefs to Washington per the request of the government. Upon their return, in gratitude for his service, the chiefs presented Abraham with a young wife, Hagar, the widow of Chief Bowlegs. Micanopy himself granted Abraham his emancipation. Although it was not formally recorded until 1835, from this point in life Abraham would consider himself free. During this period, the question of Seminole removal and emigration to the West would begin to take precedence in both the dialogue and relationships between the Seminoles and the government. As previously stated, by the 1830s, the United States government was clear on its intent to remove the Seminoles from Florida.

In 1832, when both sides agreed to meet at Payne's Landing on the Ocklawaha River located in Central Florida, Abraham was again present as interpreter and counselor to Chief Micanopy. Due to the fact that there were no minutes taken at this meeting, the actual substance of this meeting has yet to be agreed upon by historians. As far as Abraham was concerned, the United States military insisted that it had bribed Abraham with $200 to misinterpret the negotiations for removal. Initially, it would seem as if Abraham had betrayed the Seminole Indians as well as his own people.

However, if Abraham knew that the chiefs who signed the treaty had no authority to bind the entire Seminole Nation and/or the fact that the majority of the chiefs had agreed with the prior treaty which guaranteed them 20 years of payments, then what we actually discover was a cunning move of deception. When viewing the terms of the Payne's Landing Treaty, Abraham was fully aware of the fact that there were no provisions for the Black Seminoles. The fate of the Black Seminoles would therefore rest in the hands of the government and the slave society whose interests it clearly represented. To support such a treaty would mean that Abraham would have agreed to return to slavery. Not only did Abraham consistently interpret and counsel with the Black Seminole interests in mind, but also in 1833, when he accompanied the delegation of chiefs to inspect the land planned for Seminole relocation, he began to devise a plan in which Black Seminoles would obtain land and continue to live free.

Abraham, like many other members of the Black Seminoles, was once in bondage to Whites. At this point, however, he had risen in a society that allowed his abilities to flourish to the extent that he had obtained both status and respectability. He was a proven leader, demonstrating his honesty and loyalty to a community that had entrusted him with their lives. He was well aware of the consequences if the Black Seminoles returned to slavery. A lifetime of achievements would mean nothing under the plantation system. His family unit, which consisted of a wife and children, would no longer be guaranteed. Therefore, it would be quite unwise to allow the Payne's Landing Treaty to take effect, as acceptance of the treaty would result in separation from Seminole Indians. Once separated, the Black Seminoles would be vulnerable. Abraham understood that although the Black Seminoles and the Seminole Indians shared a common foe, the Black Seminoles had a much larger stake in the issue. From that point on, he deceived the United States military into thinking he was favoring peace, while he began to make preparations for a war with a different objective than his Indian counterparts.

Abraham also understood the strength of the United States military. By the 1830s, he had experienced 15 years of combat against them. He arrived at the conclusion that a concentrated effort of secret operations could offset the disparity in strength and numbers. By early 1835 and 1836, he began to build an arsenal. The preparations led by Abraham were in no way a solitary act by the Black Seminoles. Almost simultaneously, the Seminole Indians were also preparing for war. In 1834, when the government paid them their last annuity, most of the money was spent purchasing ammunition. Abraham was successful in demonstrating that the Black Seminoles' plight was related to that of the Indians, thus creating an inseparable bond.

By late 1834, Osceola successfully convinced the Seminole Indians that a united stand must be maintained. Elder members unanimously viewed migration as the demise of the Seminole Nation as a whole. Shortly thereafter, the government became fully aware of both the overall preparations for war by the unified front, as well as their implications for the removal negotiations. The government now understood that unless they directly addressed the issue of Black Seminole emigration, the emigration of the Seminole Nation would be null and void.

During the months prior to the outbreak of the Second Seminole War, Abraham sought a way to further strengthen the unified front against emigration. He also continued his efforts in preparation for war. As a tactic to accomplish both goals, Abraham began to forge stronger alliances with younger more aggressive leaders among the Indians. Abraham's diplomatic strategies, however, were not accepted. This was considerably due to his mild-mannered and good-natured demeanor. For example, it was not hard to convince Osceola of the common bond between them and the importance of unification. However, on November 26, 1835, he was unable to convince Osceola to spare the life of Chief Charley Emathla.

Abraham's hopes were that they could put up such a fight that the Seminole Indians and Black Seminoles could remain in Florida on reservations. Still, he also reconciled himself to the possibility of migration. He was uneasy about the present terms concerning migration. He knew that once they migrated westward near Creek reservations, the Creeks would attempt to subjugate the Seminole Indians and enslave the Black Seminoles, reducing them to a condition comparable to that of slavery with Whites. Therefore, the stipulations in the emigration agreement would have to ensure not only Black Seminoles' inclusion but also guarantee their safety upon arrival. Abraham never lost his loyalty to the Seminoles, however, he placed Black Seminole interests as his first priority.

Abraham was involved in the Second Seminole War from the very beginning. For the first two years of the war, he was heavily involved in fighting, strategic war planning, and negotiations. Abraham "The Prophet" occasionally stirred up the enthusiasm of Seminoles and Black Seminoles alike by utilizing religious exhortations. He prophesized the death of Gen. Wiley Thompson by stating, "He would be killed by Indians while walking about his place." Ironically enough, Thompson was killed at the beginning of the war by Osceola while strolling and smoking a cigar after his dinner.

Once the Second Seminole War began in December 1835, Abraham was, for over one year, one of the leading war-spirits. Eighty warriors were under his personal command. He would go on to garner the respect of the United States military. Its overall opinion was that Abraham was "a good soldier and intrepid leader" and "an enemy by no means to be despised." Holding true to his beliefs in secret operations, Abraham developed a hit-and-run strategy designed, as he stated, "to fly before the army and avoid a battle," taking refuge "in the dense swamps and hummocks..." of the Everglades. During the first year of the war, his strategy proved successful. He was an active participant in the ambush known as the Dade Massacre and both the First and Second Battles of the Withlacoochee.

In January 1837, his tactic of avoidance would not prove successful in the Battle of Big Cypress Swamp (the smaller of the two swamps with that name). On January 27, 1837, Abraham, as well as approximately 50 Seminoles and Black Seminoles under his command, was in the Big Cypress Swamp maneuvering to the rear side of a United States military detachment under the command of

Col. Henderson. His plan was to merge with a larger detachment of Black Seminole warriors. In the ensuing confrontation, they (the Seminoles and Black Seminoles) suffered a heavy loss. Their loss was not so much due to mortal wounds, but in persons captured and the loss of provisions. The military captured their baggage train, which contained both provisions and munitions. Also, a large number of women and children, mostly Black, were captured.

Later on, Abraham revealed that he had lost most of his personal property. He was quoted as stating, "at the Cypress...I lose most everything—all my powder and blankets, a hundred dollars in silver, pots, kettles, everything." One of Abraham's most prized possessions—his paper of manumission—was lost in battle. As a result, Abraham surrendered. In that effort, Abraham, on February 3 and February 18, 1837, successfully brought in Jumper and Alligator, along with other Seminole and Black Seminole chiefs for peace negotiations. From this point on, Abraham would be more involved in negotiations than fighting.

Abraham's involvement in the many treaty and truce negotiations throughout the years allowed him the ability to not only demonstrate his importance to the Black Seminole cause, but also his skills at negotiating on their behalf. Having long since earned the trust of the Indians, Abraham was able to maneuver his way between the two sides, creating a niche for his people. Although he stood firmly as a faithful comrade to the Seminole Indians, Abraham was never naïve enough to believe that they could defeat the United States government. However, what he did believe is that they could put forth enough resistance in order to negotiate better terms. When Abraham accompanied the delegation to view the land set aside for the Seminoles in 1833, he viewed the land itself in good favor. He would have preferred to stay in Florida on a reservation there, but the land west of the Mississippi was not a disappointment, to say the least. He consciously made a decision that Black Seminoles would also partake in this land and live free. In this instance and others, Abraham demonstrated that the leadership of the Black Seminoles had a distinct and different motive for war, compared to the leadership of the Seminoles.

In March 1836, Abraham played a pivotal role in negotiating a truce with Gen. Gaines at Camp Izard. Abraham's intent was to negotiate either a permanent arrangement or a formal treaty between the United States government and Seminole Indians that was agreeable to both sides, which stipulated that Black Seminoles would share the fate of their Seminole counterparts. Unfortunately, these negotiations, as previously discussed, ended abruptly due to a miscommunication between members of the United States military.

One year later, during negotiations in the spring, on March 6, 1837, at Camp Dade, a treaty was concluded between Gen. Jesup and the Seminole chiefs Jumper and Holatoochee (claiming to represent Micanopy). By the terms of this treaty, the Indians agreed to "cease their hostilities, come to Tampa Bay by April 10, and board the transports for the West." Furthermore, Abraham was able to negotiate the inclusion of Article V allowing Black Seminoles to emigrate. According to official military correspondence as reported in the Army and Navy Chronicle, "Major General Jesup, in behalf of the United States, agrees that the Seminole and their allies, who come in and emigrate to the west, shall be secure in their lives and property; that their Negroes their bona fide property, shall accompany them west." For Abraham, the terms "allies" and "Negroes their bona fide property" would be given the broadest of interpretations. In his mind, the struggle for the Black Seminoles' security and freedom was over. Abraham was successful in his efforts to maneuver between Seminoles and the government. The negotiations that led up to Article V were full of trickery and deceit. However, it cannot be said that his negotiations and efforts in implementing Article V did not save Black Seminole lives or ensure continued liberty.

In 1838, Abraham would work closely with Gen. Jesup in

convincing the Seminoles and Black Seminoles that emigration would secure them freedom and land. For Jesup, working closely with Abraham also represented a way to keep an eye on him, allowing direct supervision. In March 1838, Abraham, who was now considered an agent of the United States military, was successful in convincing Chief Alligator, along with his large following, to make peace. This venture was deemed a major success due to the events of April and May of 1837. Although Jesup agreed to both Article V and to protect the Black Seminoles (as long as they cooperated with emigration), pressure from slave owners caused him to rescind parts of Article V. In April 1837, Jesup issued Field Order #70 which demanded that the Seminoles yield their most recently-acquired Blacks, including those who joined them during the war. Immediately, slave owners began to appear at military posts claiming Blacks as runaways and their property. Black Seminoles and Seminoles began to leave the military posts with the intent of continuing the war.

Gen. Jesup was now in the worst situation. By May, Jesup rescinded Field Order #70 with justification as well as what he thought was a peaceful solution for both sides. He reported to the War Department that the arrival and appearance of slave owners at emigration sites caused Black Seminoles to flee. Gen. Jesup further stated, "Negroes rule them," therefore Seminoles fled too. Thus, the actions of the slave owners were the cause of the war's renewal. Jesup's solution was to allow 35 slaves to be returned to slavery, implement the original Article V, and purchase the claims of all other slave owners. Pressure was now exerted on Abraham to first regain the trust of his comrades and then convince them that they would be safe. Persuading Chief Alligator was a major accomplishment. However, Abraham would fail to convince the majority and the Second Seminole War renewed. This served as a crushing blow to both Gen. Jesup and Abraham. In July 1838, Gen. Jesup retired from the Florida campaign. As he prepared for retirement, he was successful in initiating the relocation of Abraham, his family, and 90 other Black Seminoles to Arkansas Territory.

Abraham remained loyal to his people throughout his time in Florida. Before he left Florida by way of Tampa Bay on February 25, 1839, he had the following letter sent to Gen. Jesup with his X.

> I have the honor to present my best respects to you. Tony Barnet and myself have done everything promised by us, and expect the General will do by us as he said at the beginning of this campaign...We wish to get in writing from the General the agreement made with us. We will go with the Indians to our new home, and wish to know how we are to be protected, and who is to have the care of us on the road. We do not live for ourselves only, but for our wives and children who are dear to us as those of any other men....I have charge of all the Red people coming on to Pease Creek, and all are satisfied to go to Arkansas...Whoever is to be Chief Interpreter we would wish to know. I cannot do anymore than I have. I have done all I can, my heart has been true since I came in...All Seminole Brethren are coming in...all the Black people are contented I hope. Your servant Abraham.

Although Abraham appears to have been one of the most loyal members of the Black Seminoles, unfortunately, through his negotiations with Whites (both military and otherwise), he earned many enemies. There are several ways to examine the animosities that may have arisen throughout the years. Conceivably, there were Black Seminoles, especially those who chose to dwell with their Indian counterparts, who believed that emigration was wrong and that they would rather die fighting than move. There were also those Black Seminoles who for generations had toiled and cultivated the land that they felt was theirs and believed that to negotiate any type of relocation was unthinkable.

This attachment to the land (that had been cultivated for years by their toil) would later manifest in a wider context.

For example, the same sentiments of attachment were found among Black freed-women in South Carolina just after the Civil War. The newly-emancipated expressed aspirations to own the land that they and their forefathers had toiled on for generations. From this perspective, one can perhaps understand some of their animosity towards Abraham. Perhaps Micanopy's influence had encouraged Abraham to be too concerned about negotiating for peace at times.

The fact still remains that Abraham understood that a complete victory in combat was not a realistic goal. His objective was to ensure that his people, Black Seminoles, were not forced into slavery. Therefore, when Abraham placed himself under Jesup's authority and became an agent for emigration, the question became betrayal or sacrifice. It may never be known whether all the Black Seminoles were aware of the insurmountable odds they were up against. It would seem that members of the Black Seminole community could not fully understand the complexities of negotiations during war. There may have been those within the community who simply refused to accept the mere truth—that uncompromised goals were very rarely achieved in negotiations.

Members of the Seminole Indian nation may have legitimately harbored feelings of betrayal. It is clear that from the earliest of negotiations, even before war broke out, that Abraham was reconciled to the notion of either living on reservations in Florida or emigrating west. However, given the unassertive character of Micanopy, it is also understandable how Abraham perhaps felt comfortable prioritizing the cause of the Black Seminoles, whether it coincided with the Seminole cause or not. Abraham very well may have manipulated Micanopy, as others did, for his own agenda.

Many historians would agree with the assertion that Abraham utilized the fondness and trust of Micanopy as a license to negotiate on the behalf of his people. Micanopy's fondness for the Black Seminoles may have given Abraham the authority to negotiate as he did without the consent of other chiefs. Therefore, it is safe to say that as an interpreter and negotiator, he did not fully serve all the interests of the Seminole Indians at all times. Still, the crux of the matter is whether the Indians fared better by emigrating as opposed to facing near annihilation through continued armed resistance. One could argue that the Seminoles would have emigrated eventually, whether it was in 1832 with the Payne's Landing Treaty or with the ending of the war. However, the provisions and dignity with which they emigrated in 1842 would not have been so in 1832.

If there were any flaws in Abraham's thinking or actions during his time spent in Florida and especially during the Second Seminole War, it was his naïve trust that Gen. Jesup's decisions were supreme and not subject to rejection by a higher authority. While in Washington, had not Abraham observed and understood the hierarchical structure of the government? Did he not recognize the authority of those he met there? Was he led to believe that Gen. Jesup had the full cooperation of the government? I contend that Abraham was led to believe that the decisions made by Gen. Jesup would be accepted and guaranteed by those in Washington. Not until after Field Order #70 did Abraham completely understand that Gen. Jesup's authority was not absolute. Furthermore, this was the basis upon which his relationship with Gen. Jesup developed. The relationship in itself was still an adversarial one. Nevertheless, his trust in Gen. Jesup relied upon his authority in the war.

The first few years of Abraham's life after his emigration are not clear. However, it is known that conflicts between the Creeks and the Seminoles increased the suffering of Black Seminoles. As suspected by Abraham years prior to emigration, Creek Indians would begin to lay claims on Black Seminoles as runaway slaves. In 1845, Abraham was a witness to a treaty that sought to rectify the bad relations between Creeks and Seminoles. The sudden death of Micanopy in 1848 worsened the position of the Black Seminoles out west. Micanopy's successor, Jim Jumper, sought peaceful coexistence with the Creeks through appeasement.

After 1845, Abraham's life seems to have fallen into obscurity. It is believed that Abraham was among the Black Seminoles who migrated, in September 1850, across Texas into Mexico with Seminole comrades. In 1852, men who were guarding the United States commissioners, while establishing the Mexican border, were taken by Seminoles to their village where Abraham was living and still respected as a leader.

Abraham's life signifies a life of charisma, leadership and struggle. From his youth, Abraham sought freedom. Freedom from slavery would become a lifelong endeavor in which he sought liberty not only for himself but also for all Black Seminoles. Whether one agrees with the decisions that he made throughout the various conflicts, one cannot question his dedication to his people. His intent was clear from his earliest beginnings as an interpreter and sense bearer. There is no doubt that he was a devout abolitionist in his own right.

John Caesar

The majority of John Caesar's life is quite obscure. In fact, the known information about John Caesar covers a period of just over a year (December 1835–January 1837). This is primarily due to the limited contact between John Caesar and Whites (whether they be military or otherwise) in the territory. This observation, however, by no means diminishes his importance, contributions or leadership during the Second Seminole War.

John Caesar was described as short and stocky with a broad face. He was generally believed to have been an elderly man at the advent of the war, probably in his late 50s or 60s. Caesar was one of the Black Seminoles who for the better part of his life lived directly in the company of Seminoles. His mastery of English suggests either an early childhood in plantation society or rearing by slave parents. Whatever the case, he became a "slave" of Chief Emathla (or King Philip as Whites called him), the principal chief of the St. Johns River Seminoles. In time, Caesar became Emathla's counselor, interpreter and commander of the Black Seminoles under his protection, a relationship identical to Abraham's relationship with Micanopy.

Chief Emathla was described as a man inclined to peace but unwilling to relocate and determined to live and die in Florida. Basically Chief Emathla was more inclined to negotiations and peaceful co-existence with Whites in Florida. However, if the United States government was adamant about forcing his removal, the chief was willing to go to war.

Chief Emathla's policy of conflict avoidance is most likely the reason why so little information is known about Caesar. In all likelihood, Caesar adhered to this policy whenever possible. Therefore, most of John Caesar's life will continue to be embedded in mystery and clouded by rumors and speculation. As for Chief Emathla, he would go on to discover that the government would not entertain any thought of peaceful coexistence with the Seminoles in the Florida Territory.

In the fall of 1837, for reasons unknown, four runaways returned to the custody of the Whites. They brought with them John Philip who, under pressure from his wife, had grown weary of the hardships of war. John Philip agreed to guide the military to a Seminole encampment. In September, Gen. Joseph M Hernandez was led to an encampment just south of St. Augustine on the Tomoka River. In a surprise attack, Emathla was found by the river bathing. He was captured and taken into the custody of Gen. Thomas S. Jesup. As an elderly man who wished to live the rest of his life in peace, the chief agreed to emigrate. He requested a visit by his son and closest friends. During this visit, he convinced his son to speak to the other chiefs about a peaceful surrender. Unfortunately, in the following year (1838), the chief died during his emigration trip.

Caesar was regarded by Whites as very intelligent, an actively smart Negro, and next to Abraham in influence and importance among the Seminoles. During the Second Seminole War, he was a primary instigator of plantation slaves, a principal leader of plantation raids, interpreter, negotiator, diplomat, and overall Black Seminole leader. His position within both communities, Seminole and Black Seminole, is magnified when compared to the actual amount of time in which he participated in the war.

While Abraham is noted as the Black Seminole primarily responsible for the development of the secret network between plantation slaves and Black Seminoles, Caesar was the individual most responsible for establishing the ties between the two. This most likely was due to the fact that Caesar's wife was a plantation slave. Not only was he known to frequently visit her plantation but also several plantations in the area. It has been noted that because of this close connection, it became easy for Abraham and Caesar to visit plantations to meet with slaves in attempts to incite them to insurrection in cooperation with their cause.

In time, plantation owners would come to realize that an understanding between their slaves and the Seminoles had developed. This understanding was created by the Black Seminoles with an underlying promise of freedom. There is no doubt that this "inducement" related to promises of freedom. However, it seems that emphatic guarantees would not have been necessary. Caesar himself would have been verification. If slaves were doubtful about their life outside of the plantation, they would need to look no further than Caesar, a man who periodically visited them while seeming to come and go as he pleased. If indeed they had concerns about the idea of exchanging a White master for a Red one, the lifestyle of Caesar perhaps enticed them to believe that they would still be elevating their station in life. Furthermore, the meetings themselves were planned with those slaves on the plantation who were already recognized as leaders within their respective communities. Influence over a number of these slaves could conceivably result in influence among the enslaved population in general.

Caesar's relationship with the plantation slaves represented an enormous threat to plantation society in the Florida Territory. In the years just prior to the Second Seminole War, Whites and Blacks in Florida were almost equal in number. According to the 1830 population census, there were approximately 18,000 Whites and 16,000 enslaved Blacks in the Florida Territory. These numbers do not include the Seminole population nor do they include the Black Seminole population. As tensions increased between plantation society and the Seminoles, White Floridians began to pressure the government for protection.

To counter Caesar's efforts towards unification, Whites began to pass laws to discourage free Blacks from arming themselves and uniting with the Seminoles. In July 1836, a bill was passed stipulating that any free Black that aided the Seminoles in any way would be sold into slavery. A massive slave rebellion within plantation society ultimately would have meant that Whites would have had to fight two wars simultaneously, a war against the Seminoles and an internal war against the slaves. As if to confirm the Whites' worst fears, approximately 400 slaves fled the plantations to join the Seminoles by January 1836.

In December 1835, Caesar assumed a leadership position in the attacks upon plantations in the area located around the St. Johns River. The first casualty of the plantation raids under his leadership was the house of David Dunham located in New Smyrna, south of Mosquito Inlet. Dunham's house was "plundered and burned." It was a collective effort involving Chief Emathla's Seminoles and Black Seminoles under Caesar's command. Days later, Caesar appeared at Mr. Hunter's residence and attempted to lure him off into the woods under the pretense of selling cattle and horses. Mr. Hunter was apparently too suspicious of Caesar's actions and cautiously declined, probably saving his own life.

The raid at Dunham's struck a blow at plantation society in two ways. It destroyed a plantation, physically causing economic woe, and aided in the recruitment of slaves. Although the Hunter attempt failed, it was nevertheless deemed a success in that it encouraged slaves to join the Seminole effort. It was reported in newspapers that "Depeyster's negroes were…in league with the Indians; they assisted them with a vote to cross over to Dummetts'…Upwards of two hundred fifty negroes…have joined the Indians and are more desperate than the Indians." Evidently, once the slaves began to witness the resistance of the Seminoles and Black Seminoles, they became keener to secure their own freedom. Runaway slaves put paint on their faces as a symbol of their allegiance to the Seminole cause. The threat of unification was now a clear danger to the military, as well as to other Whites who resided in the Florida Territory. Brig. Gen. JM Hernandez candidly recognized the perils of unification, stating, "[it] is the very worse feature of the whole of this war." Later, he would go on to recognize the leadership of Caesar during the events, asserting that he had "caused so much destruction…"

For a brief period, just after the plantation raids in December, Caesar disappeared from public view. It would seem that for approximately two months Caesar adhered to the avoidance policy. However, this very well may have been adherence to Abraham's tactics of guerilla warfare where they would attack the enemy suddenly, then retreat into the dense forest. In either case, Caesar appeared at the siege of Fort Izard on March 5, 1836. He was an active participant in the negotiations. That night, Caesar was said to have contacted Gen. Gaines, declaring that the Indians were tired of fighting and wanted peace. This was done without the authority of the Indian chiefs. Thus, the other chiefs wanted to kill him but his life was spared only through Osceola's intervention.

Caesar was negotiating with two agendas in mind. He still adhered to the policy of his Seminole chief, which called for peaceful cohabitation with Whites and all Seminoles in the territory. His attacks on nearby plantations in December may have been no more than an obligatory act of retaliation against the encroachment of plantation society on their communities, as opposed to a general declaration of war. This is based on the fact that he did not participate in any other conflict outside of the St. Johns River region for two months. Additionally, Caesar adhered to the strategy of Abraham in regard to actively participating in negotiations for terms that included the Black Seminoles. He did not go to Camp Izard solely as a representative of his chief. Instead, he also took it upon himself to go as a Black Seminole chief representing the Black Seminoles in the St. Johns River region.

Furthermore, it is my contention that when Osceola spoke up for Caesar and defended him, it was a significant gesture that suggested that Seminole chiefs were now recognizing Black Seminoles as an independent group and no longer merely a group of individuals under their protection. This idea is supported by the events following Osceola's intervention on Caesar's behalf. The next day, two conferences were held to outline future war strategies and both Abraham and Caesar were present. The fact that neither Micanopy nor Emathla was present implies that Abraham and Caesar were there merely as representatives. However, none of the elderly Seminole chiefs were present. By 1836, the younger chiefs were taking the leadership positions in the war effort and seemed to accept the Black Seminoles as an independent and equal ally. Therefore, Abraham and Caesar very well may have been representing their Seminole chiefs but they were primarily there representing the interests of the Black Seminoles.

After the conference, Caesar once again disappeared from the public view for over ten months. It is believed that he returned to the St. Johns River region. Toward the end of 1836, he was recognized for aiding the efforts of Chief Emathla to repel the South Carolina volunteers around the St. Johns River. Here again, when actual warfare was concerned, Caesar actively maintained the policy of avoidance whenever possible. He constantly maintained this balance between the philosophies of Abraham and Chief Emathla.

In December of the same year, things would change in a manner that would no longer allow Caesar to maintain this balance. A new commander in chief, Maj. Gen. Thomas S. Jesup, entered Florida and zealously swept across the frontier. Consequently, the Alachua Seminoles and Black Seminoles were driven eastward in the direction of the St. Johns River region. Caesar realized the policy of avoidance would allow the Alachua Seminoles to be defeated and it would only be a matter of time before the United States military would approach the St. Johns region. Therefore, he began a guerilla campaign primarily utilizing runaway slaves. His campaign consisted of a few bands operating under his command. Each band is believed to have consisted of approximately 12 men. Caesar's band, at his last recorded raid, consisted of eight runaway slaves, a free Black, two Seminoles, and two Black Seminoles who most likely belonged to his group of Black Seminoles in the St. Johns region.

In January 1837, Caesar began to garner the necessities needed for the campaign. In mid-January, he and his band attempted to raid John M Hanson's plantation just west of St. Augustine. There, they would attempt to steal horses from the stable. In the process of creating a large enough opening to lead the animals out, they were discovered by a sentinel. Gunfire was exchanged. Although there were no casualties, the night watch in St. Augustine was alerted. Consequently, Caesar and his raiders withdrew. The next day, the military followed their trail. At approximately 10 pm, the military discovered the band's encampment about 30 miles from St. Augustine on the Williams' plantation. The military proceeded to sneak into the encampment. Once they got close enough, they opened fire and created such a panic that many simply fled, leaving behind ammunition, guns and supplies. As a result, three members of the band were killed, while at least one was badly wounded. Two of the three killed were Black Seminoles from the St. Johns River region. One of them was John Caesar himself. He was identified by his distinguished clothing. The Seminole cause had lost one of its most outstanding warriors. Likewise, the Black Seminoles had lost one of their most influential and distinguished leaders.

The effect of Caesar's raid was felt by Gen. Jesup, as well as White residents in the vicinity. Days later, Gen. Jesup won two major battles at Hatcheelustee and in the Great Cyprus Swamp. It would seem that Jesup viewed the month of January as a major success and therefore decided to press harder. However, in March 1837, Article V of the Articles of Capitulation was adopted. Moreover, the makeup of Caesar's band alone demonstrated the solidarity of Seminoles, Black Seminoles, free Blacks outside the Black Seminole community, and those enslaved; this undoubtedly had to have had an enormous effect on Jesup as he began to seek out favorable terms for peace to end the war.

As previously mentioned, the greatest fear of the military was to have to fight the Second Seminole War, while also suppressing a major slave insurrection. It is my contention that Caesar's raid induced Gen. Jesup to include Article V. Jesup undoubtedly understood that the relationship between Black Seminoles and plantation slaves was strengthening as the war progressed. The longer the war lasted, the more slaves gained confidence in the Seminoles' cause and were more willing to join. Gen. Jesup was in the process of seeking a way to somehow separate the Seminoles from the Black Seminoles. Caesar's band represented the very worst scenario: a unification of all groups in the territory against the Whites. Therefore, despite the death of Caesar and the victories at Hatcheelustee and in the Great Cypress Swamp, Jesup offered the Black Seminoles favorable terms for peace.

Although the death of Caesar came as a relief to Whites in the Florida Territory, especially those in the St. Johns River region, his attempted raid caused much concern. Whites were alarmed by the fact that the band was almost entirely made up of Blacks. The mere fact that Blacks would be daring and bold enough to attempt a deed almost entirely on their own sent shock waves through the White community. Up until this point, in terms of warfare, Blacks were basically believed to only be misled by Indians into calculated acts. The most alarming fact about Blacks participating in the raid was that when Whites searched the belongings left by the fleeing band, they discovered numerous articles, such as calico, needles, thread, buckshot and tobacco, which were identified as being purchased in the shops of St. Augustine. This demonstrated a relationship with Blacks in the city.

As a result of both fear and panic, it was believed that Blacks in St. Augustine would set fire to the city, enabling the Seminoles to besiege it. In response to the alarm, the city council was convinced that their slaves were in cooperation with the Seminoles against them and demanded that the military remain with them for protection and pursue others who may be among them. In light of Caesar's raid, Whites quickly made a correlation between the Second Seminole War and a slave rebellion within their society. In essence, the Second Seminole War convinced Whites of the dire need to separate their slaves from the Black Seminoles (the majority of who were runaway slaves) in hopes of not having a massive rebellion throughout the Florida Territory.

The most significant contributions of John Caesar were his ability to unify the Seminole cause with Blacks in the plantation areas and provide leadership to those who joined the Seminole cause. Without the assistance of slaves and free Blacks, the Seminole cause would not have been as successful in garnering the necessities needed for fighting the campaign nor would they have been as successful in infiltrating plantations in the territory. Caesar incited and inspired many slaves to no longer simply tolerate their station in life as oppressed servants. He went on to provide leadership to those slaves who were willing to seize an opportunity to gain their freedom.

Under the influence and leadership of Caesar, plantation slaves assumed principal roles in contesting territory from the St. Johns River region up to the city of St. Augustine. They were also responsible for keeping Whites in the region in terror during the early years of the Second Seminole War. Those runaway slaves who stayed in close contact with Caesar (primarily those in his particular band) would go on to assume other leadership positions within the slave communities. The most notable members of those runaway slaves in his band were Andrew Gu'e (or Gay), Stephen Hernandez, Philip Hunter, John Bicente, Toney Weightman, Hector Anderson, Benet Depeyster, and Ormond Depeyster. Of those listed, Andrew Gu'e and Stephen Hernandez were the most noteworthy.

Andrew Gu'e is credited with being the most prominent of runaway slaves. He was described at the time of the war as "a young negro, not exceeding twenty-one years of age, and active and enterprising." It was reported that "He went off, joined the Indians, and after being with them for some weeks, he returned clandestinely to town and held a meeting with some of his friends, and encouraged some of them off. At this meeting he stated that he had become high in the confidence of the Indians and he only wanted a white man's scalp to make him a great man." The report goes on further to tell the story of how he was once captured with other Black Seminoles but escaped and "on several occasions since made his appearance in the vicinity." Gu'e took on an active leadership role in the interaction between Black Seminoles and Blacks within plantation society. After the failed raid with Caesar, Gu'e was later captured and placed in United States military custody. From that point on, he seems to have disappeared from the historical record.

Stephen Hernandez was a slave of Gen. Joseph L Hernandez. He ran away to join the Seminole cause while Gen. Hernandez was commanding the Florida militia in the St. Augustine area. When notified that Stephen had run away and was actively participating in the war, Gen. Hernandez remarked, "Stephen…is quite a young and inexperienced lad, who has always been kept up on the plantation, and I have no doubt, he has been misled, by his Indian associates." The information that Stephen would be able to give to the Black Seminoles would be instrumental in creating strategy. His importance within the Black Seminole community would eventually elevate him to a position of leadership.

Caesar's contact with free Blacks within plantation society proved to be instrumental to the acquisition of supplies. Free Blacks arranged these purchases of supplies and provided valuable information on the movements of the military between various plantations. There were two noted free Blacks who were especially crucial to these operations. They perhaps should be viewed as true champions of the cause of freedom in that they were already free but were willing to take greater risks than most free Blacks for the sake of liberty for their fellow Blacks in the region. These two free Blacks were Randal Irving and Joe Merritt.

Although Randal Irving never officially became a member of the Black Seminole community, he was quite instrumental in providing Black Seminoles with supplies and ammunition purchased from Spanish traders. Irving resided on Anastasia Island just off the Florida coast. Irving's location alone provided an ideal meeting place. In preparation for a raid, three members of Caesar's band (John Bicente, Joe Merritt and Andrew Gu'e) met with Irving. At this meeting, Irving supplied them with provisions and ammunition. After the failed raid, Irving was placed on trial for treason against the United States. During the trial, he testified to the number of participants in Caesar's band and that Caesar himself was among them waiting for the supplies. During Irving's arrest and trial, he became ill. It is not known whether he was executed or died in custody, but there is no record of his enslavement.

Joe Merritt was also a free Black and resident of Anastasia Island. He was believed to have been a young man during the war, possibly in his mid to late teens. Nevertheless, Joe became a liaison between free Blacks and Black Seminoles. He was directly under the mentorship of Caesar. How he became a member of his band is not exactly known. During the trials of free Blacks in the region, a story was told that Caesar and Joe's father, Stephen Merritt, had quarreled over money that was supposedly owed by Stephen to Caesar. As a result, Caesar got Joe. Whether this was indeed the case or Joe joined Caesar of his own accord is unknown. What is known is that Joe was actively involved with Caesar and participated in the meeting with Randall for supplies. Joe also participated in Caesar's raid and was with him when his encampment was discovered. As a result, Joe was one of the three killed along with Caesar.

Although key members of the band were subdued, the Second Seminole War would continue for another five years after John Caesar's death; his contributions would be a principal factor in not only the creation of Article V, but also its implementation in 1842. Caesar was the primary agent instigating a war that encompassed the regions outside of the plantation zone as well as inside. By forging a union with free Blacks and slaves in Florida's plantation system, Caesar incorporated a slave revolt and partisan warfare, as well as a significant supply line for the Seminole cause throughout the entire war. Porter contends that if there was any weakness of John Caesar it was his recklessness, which resulted in his death. I contend that this recklessness was not a weakness but actually his assertiveness, once he made a conscious decision to not adhere to Chief Emathla's avoidance policy.

The task of unification was in itself an undertaking that demanded action and was unachievable through diplomacy alone. In order to gain their active support, slaves needed to witness defiance against their masters. More Whites were murdered during the Second Seminole War than during any other time in Antebellum Florida. Caesar's frequent visits and exhortation speeches to slaves incited them to flee to the Seminoles. His recklessness jolted plantation slaves into rebellion. There was no other way for Caesar to incite rebellion on a massive scale than to proceed with reckless abandonment. The fact that between 1835 and 1837 more than 400 slaves fled their respective plantations to join the Seminole cause, with less than 50 percent returned to Whites, demonstrates the effectiveness of Caesar's actions. Caesar understood that unification was the only way, and for that he gave his life.

John Cavallo

When examining the contributions of Abraham and John Caesar, one may get the impression that the leadership role of Black Seminoles during the war was short-lived. John Cavallo's leadership during the Second Seminole War suggests just the opposite. Of all the Black Seminoles who participated in the war, no other person served a greater length of time nor had more contact with Whites before, during or after the war. Consequently, there is more information available on his life than on any other Black Seminole.

John Cavallo (also known as Gopher John, John Cowaya and John Horse) was born around 1812. He was the product of a union between Seminole Chief Charles Cavallo (also known as Imotley) and a Black woman. Given his father's association with the Alachua Seminoles and his relationship with Chief Alligator, it can be deduced that he was born in the Alachua Seminole heartland near present-day Gainesville and Lake City. In this region, the Seminoles were primarily agriculturalists and reared large herds of cattle. As a result of the Patriot War, Chief Cavallo moved the tribe approximately 12 miles northeast of present-day Tampa Bay, close to Lake Thonotosassa. It is here that John spent most of his youth.

Chief Cavallo's settlement for the most part prospered during young John's life. It was well situated in close proximity to the American Post at Fort Brooke. In 1823, just after the Treaty of Moultrie Creek, the military established Fort Brooke in order to provide administrative assistance to Seminoles on reservations, while supervising their activities. Existing trails allowed Seminoles to travel to the military post and prosper through trade. Seminoles often sold turkey, venison and whooping crane.

Although much is not recorded about John prior to the war, there is one story from his youth that offers a glimpse of his intelligence and brave demeanor. It is also the story of how he became known as Gopher John. George McCall, stationed at Fort Brooke in 1826, recalled:

> A long-legged, lathy negro boy of some fourteen years, belonging to one of the Thlonoto-sasa Indians, called at this officer's quarters and offered for sale a brace of gophers. He received his quarter of a dollar; and Andrew, the cook, a negro slave, was ordered to put them in the crawl, which at that time happened to be empty. He was also charged to feed them regularly with dried beans and other articles of vegetable diet. The next day the boy, John, brought another pair of gophers to the same officer, and received his quarter. The next day it was the same, and the next, and the next. The officer was delighted with his good fortune, and at the end of some ten days, not having kept the count strictly, he told Andrew to count the gophers, and let him know how many were in the crawl. Andrew did go to the crawl, in one corner of which a quantity of brush had been thrown, under which these *nocturnal* animals might retire during the day; and he did shake up the brush and toss it about very thoroughly, but he saw never a gopher but the two he had just put in.
>
> Andrew, naturally enough, was first amazed, then perplexed, and finally confounded at the discovery he had made; for he could be sworn he had daily put a brace into the crawl for many days in succession; and so he protested to his master to whom he hastened with the news.
>
> His master was no less surprised than Andrew; and in addition he was first disappointed, then vexed, and finally enraged at the cheat he began to suspect had been played upon him. He at once sent out his *Orderly* to look for Master John, who was soon brought before him, looking as pale as a negro can look. Under the fear of being well flogged if he did not confess, John let out

the truth; which of course was, that he had leaped the paling
every night and captured the gophers he had sold during the day
before.

John escaped punishment that day but was left with the name
"Gopher John." From this point on, he would go on to have numerous
interactions with the Americans, becoming more acquainted with
the United States military as a whole. In turn, the military had no
idea that the young boy they jokingly called Gopher John would
become one of their most formidable adversaries during the War.

In just a short period, the existing trails that provided the
Seminole and Black Seminole villages' access to other inhabited
areas in the region became one of the focal points in the rising
tensions between the Seminoles and Whites inhabiting the western
peninsular region. The northward expansion of these trails became
viewed by White settlers as an enticement for runaways to the
peninsula. At the same time, plantation society in the Florida
Panhandle increasingly encroached upon Seminole communities.
Whites in this region were demanding the removal of both
Seminoles and Black Seminoles. The mounting tensions caused a
ripple effect, such that more Seminoles and Black Seminoles began
traveling the trails that led to Chief Cavallo's settlement in search of
both trade in the peninsula, as well as a respite from the encroaching
plantation society. By the end of 1826, an army official estimated
that Thonotosassa's population had reached 200.

Young John grew up in the midst of the village's growth and,
with his father's ever-increasing importance, he began to encounter
and eventually develop relationships with key Seminole leaders. It is
certain that during this period of his life he became well acquainted
with Chief Alligator, a principal chief who resided to the east of
Thonotosassa on the Peace River (also known as Pease Creek).
In time, John would go on to develop a relationship with Chief
Alligator which resembled the relationship between Abraham and
Micanopy, as well as John Caesar's relationship with Chief Emathla.

It can also be assumed that at some point during John's youth he resided along the Peace River, most likely in the company of Chief Alligator, due to the fact that during the early stages of the war some military officers knew him as Pease Creek John.

During the first year of the Second Seminole War, John Cavallo's specific activities and contributions are not known. However, the war started around the region of Fort Brooke and Lake Thonotosassa, which suggests that he may have been involved in the fighting. Gen. Winfield Scott's forces invaded the Peace River frontier, destroying villages and encampments. In May 1836, one of the bloodiest battles fought during the war occurred close to Lake Thonotosassa. Most likely it is during this period that John Cavallo allied with Chief Alligator and Chief Osceola, as they became the principal Seminole war chiefs in the regions surrounding Tampa Bay leading up to Alachua. Also, John probably became the Black Seminole leader most active in efforts to unify the Black Seminoles and plantation slaves of the Florida Territory's western frontier. He is believed to have participated in the Dade Massacre, as well as the battles at Withlacoochee and Wahoo Swamp. It is during this period (1835–1836) that John was beginning to transform into an intrepid Black Seminole war chief known throughout the Florida Territory.

In the spring of 1837, John Cavallo was recognized by the United States military as a Black Seminole leader and references to him in a leadership capacity were presumably first made by Gen. Jesup in February when he stated, "Abraham has just come in with a flag, accompanied by a nephew of the Indian Chief Cloud, and a negro chief." It can be assumed that the "negro chief" Gen. Jesup refers to was John Cavallo, due to the fact that the only other Black Seminole given the responsibility of participating in negotiations was John Caesar. It could not have been Caesar, as he was killed the month prior to the negotiations (January). In March, John represented Chief Alligator at the negotiations that resulted in the inclusion of Article V. There, he signed the peace treaty on

Alligator's behalf. From this point on, he would be recognized as Chief Alligator's sense bearer or adviser. In reference to the Black Seminoles, Gen. Jesup recognized John Cavallo as a principal chief.

As a result of the negotiations, John Cavallo agreed to emigration and began preparations for departure. On March 7, 1837, he was placed in Gen. Jesup's custody. The next month he was relocated to an emigrating camp near Fort Brooke. During April, he was released for a short period in order to get his affairs in order. John would begin to assume more responsibilities, thus enhancing his leadership role among the Seminoles and especially the Black Seminoles.

In compliance with the agreement he made during negotiations to protect Black Seminoles from Whites trying to reclaim slaves, Gen. Jesup barred access to any unauthorized Whites to any part of the territory, between the St. Johns River and the Gulf of Mexico. Gen. Jesup stated that he had "reason to believe that the interference of unprincipled white men with the negro property of the Seminole Indians if not immediately checked will prevent their emigration and lead to a renewal of the war." Gen. Jesup was well aware of the rising tension between Whites and Seminoles in the territory. He was also well aware of the adamant nature in which Whites pursued runaway slaves. The loss of one or two slaves could result in the financial ruin of a White farmer. More slaves were brought in to counter the loss of slaves and continue the growth of plantation society prior to the war. The growth of the Black population during this time period was primarily due to the expansion of plantation society in Middle Florida and the loss of slaves during the war.

Gen. Jesup's assumptions proved to be correct. Whites immediately began to swarm Fort Brooke with claims of ownership of runaway slaves. In the midst of the confusion, John escaped. Gen. Jesup recalled, "Jumper and Abraham came in with a message from Micanopy…He sent word that John Cowaya had stolen five of our horses, and had runaway with all his people."

Gen. Jesup was enraged; he immediately ordered the incarceration of all Black Seminoles. In June, John returned to Fort Brooke with Osceola and approximately 200 warriors. They besieged the fort and escaped with approximately 700 Seminoles and Black Seminoles. As a result of the siege and rescue, the Second Seminole War resumed. Gen. Jesup then reported to his supervisor, "This campaign so far as relates to Indian migration has entirely failed."

Gen. Jesup's initial reaction to the siege on Fort Brooke was that of disheartened despair and frustration, but his feelings quickly transformed into revenge. His first tactical maneuver was to authorize the volunteer forces to capture Black Seminoles and retain them as slaves. He began to consider using bloodhounds to track Black Seminoles. His general policy towards Blacks involved in the war was to capture them and treat them all as runaway slaves. As a tactic to sever the bond between the Seminole Indians and the Black Seminoles, he began to entertain the idea of offering those Indians who vehemently opposed migration a reservation in the territory. It is clear that Gen. Jesup and the United States military viewed the Seminole Indians and the Black Seminoles as two distinct groups. The inclusion of Article V was their first acknowledgement of this view. Gen. Jesup offered peaceable negotiations to the Black Seminoles in order to rupture their alliance with the Seminoles and end the war. Now, Gen. Jesup, utterly dissatisfied with John Cavallo, entertained the idea of negotiating with the Seminole Indians in the hopes of ending the war, while exacting vengeance upon the Black Seminoles.

After the siege and rescue at Fort Brooke, Micanopy led the majority of the band eastward to the Kissimmee River where they erected an encampment. John was placed in charge of the group. His following consisted of only 15 Seminole Indians and an unidentified number of Blacks. The division of the occupants was based primarily on the Indian/Black ratio. Therefore, this division was yet another example of the military's distinctions made between the Seminole Indians and Black Seminoles. Micanopy was the chief in charge of the Seminole Indians and after the emigration of Abraham, John Horse was the chief in charge of the Black Seminoles.

As a response to the escape at Fort Brooke, Gen. Jesup devised a broad campaign directed at the Seminole strongholds. Jesup believed that the Black Seminoles were encamped west of the Kissimmee River in the upper Peace River area. The military erected Fort Fraser just north of present-day Bartow to gain access to the Peace River. Col. Zachary Taylor was then instructed to lead a large contingent from Fort Brooke to the Kissimmee River. Jesup's orders clearly identify the distinction he made between the two groups as different directives were given for each.

As it turns out, Jesup was correct in calculating the position of the Seminole Indians. However, John and Chief Alligator had joined Micanopy at his encampment. John was ordered by both chiefs to find Chief Osceola and Coacoochee (also known as Wild Cat), consult with them, and serve as their interpreter if necessary. In October, Coacoochee was captured by Jesup, along with others under his command. With the loss of his closest ally in the region, Osceola called for a parley, to which Jesup responded, "On the 20th [October], John Cavallo, a sub-chief, a hostage who had violated his parole in May of last year, came into St. Augustine with a message from [Osceola] and Coa Hajo, stating that they had encamped near the fort, and desired to see General Hernandez. I…required General Hernandez to seize them, and take them to St. Augustine." Jesup goes further to warn them "that wherever John Cavallo was, foul play might be expected."

In compliance with Jesup's orders, Hernandez took Osceola, John Horse and over 72 others into custody, arresting and jailing them in St. Augustine's Castillo de San Marcos with Coacoochee. Hernandez encountered Osceola and Coa Hajo standing under a white flag of truce. Present at the encounter was assistant surgeon

Nathan Jarvis who recalled:

> On our arrival at their camp we discovered at a short distance
> by a white flag flying the Indians immediately gathered around
> us shaking hands with all the officers. My attention was of
> course first directed to discover Os-Cin-Ye-hola [Osceola]. He
> was soon pointed out to me but I could have designated him by
> his looks as the principal man among them. Nothing of savage
> fierceness or determination marked his countenance, on the
> contrary his features indicated mildness and benevolence.
> A continued smile played over his face, particularly when
> shaking hands with the officers present.

Hernandez (through an interpreter) asked them, "Have you
come to give up to me as your friend?" Coa Hajo replied, "No, we
did not understand so word went from here, and we have come we
have done nothing all summer, and we want to make peace." After
more conversation Hernandez gave the signal and the troops moved
in. Four Black Seminoles were among those taken into custody
(including John Cavallo). They were all marched between two lines
of soldiers and into custody. This would be the second time that
John was taken into custody. Unlike the first, he was considered
a prisoner charged with breaking a truce. However, like the first,
John would escape yet again. His participation is never specifically
outlined in any of the accounts of the night of November 29 when he
and Coacoochee escaped. However, John's actions can be outlined
based upon available sources.

There are numerous conflicting accounts of the escape,
including a story told by Coacoochee himself. The news of the
escape spread like wildfire. One officer reported, "Indians mostly
Mikisukis headed by that daring rascal Co-oor-coo-chy and John
Cavallo escaped from Fort St Marks." He went on further to state,
"If they get down among the Indians, good bye to peace this year
at least…General J[esup] is much cast down by this occurrence."
Jesup himself declared, "John Cowaggee…is the greatest rascal in
the nation except Alligator." For Jesup, the escape would be the least

of his problems at the time.

Jesup could not have imagined the national attention that would arise from the arrest of Chief Osceola who, due to illness, a defeated spirit or a combination of the two, decided not to join the escape. Osceola had become a martyr in American popular opinion. In 1838, Jesup found himself on the floor of Congress defending his actions with only half of the legislators supporting him. After all, he did arrest them under a truce flag. Those in support of Jesup offered six reasons to justify his actions. They were:

1. Osceola had not kept his word in agreement to emigrate.

2. Osceola and Coa Hadjo returned to St. Augustine to rescue Chief Emathla and massacre Whites.

2. Osceola agreed to parley knowing that Jesup had refused further negotiations.

3. Jesup claimed that Osceola killed a messenger under a truce flag.

4. The Seminole Indians had broken the truce in August 1837 by committing hostile acts.

6. Osceola's arrest was warranted in the need for expediency in the war.

The justifications proved adequate as Jesup returned to the war with his command still intact. However, the arrest of Osceola under a truce flag would leave an indelible mark on his military career which he spent years trying to erase. In 1858, 20 years after the affair, Jesup submitted this excerpt from a letter to a Washington newspaper.

A matter has recently been brought into discussion which my name was connected some twenty years ago, and though explained at the time, seems not even now to be well understood. It has been published in a neighboring print on the authority of a distinguished professional and public man that the Seminole Indian Warrior Osceola who by the murder of General Thompson and other atrocities started the Seminole War, was captured by treachery and fraud.

As a result of the escape, Jesup went on a relentless pursuit of John and Coacoochee who were en route to join Alligator encamped around Lake Okeechobee. In his bitterness, Jesup first threatened Emathla with death if they did not give themselves up. He would rescind this threat a day or two later once he calmed down. In order to pursue the escapees and confront Alligator at Lake Okeechobee, Jesup assembled the largest army mobilized during the Second Seminole War. Utilizing all the available military aid including volunteers, Jesup marched approximately 9,000 men in pursuit.

On Christmas Day 1837, Gen. Taylor received word that John's brother-in-law had been captured and had informed them that a large body of Seminoles, headed by John Co-hua [John Cavallo], Co-a-coo-chee, Alligator, and other chiefs, were encamped five or six miles away, near the Mikasukies. Outnumbering the Seminoles by a margin of about two to one, Taylor engaged them in battle. After approximately two-and-a-half hours, the battle ended, leaving 26 United States soldiers dead and 112 wounded. The Seminoles suffered 11 deaths and 14 wounded. The Seminoles would sustain a heavier loss overall, since large amounts of food and supplies were lost. The combined forces of the Seminole Nation retreated further south and west. Taylor withdrew northward to Fort Basinger, while Jesup began approaching the region from the Atlantic coast.

By 1838, both sides were growing weary of war. The losses suffered during the battle at Lake Okeechobee by the Seminoles proved to be more than some members could bear. Jesup, too, was growing weary. In February, Jesup took an official position to allow the Indians to remain in Florida and in his own words, he was "determined to separate all the negroes from the Indians and send them out of the country as soon as possible."

In April, Alligator and John capitulated, after Jesup sent word that John was promised his freedom and protection. Jesup reported, "Alligator, one of the most active and warlike of the hostiles, had surrendered at Fort Basinger on the 4th of April. He was found with 88 of his people, among whom were John Cowaya and 27 blacks, to the southwest of Okeechobee. Alligator was to return to his party, and, by means of runners, collect all the scattered Indians, and concentrate them at Peace Creek." John arrived on April 14. Abraham was instrumental in bringing him in under peaceful conditions.

It was befitting that John's departure from Florida that June took place in the region of his youth. During his emigration, he first went to Fort Fraser on the Peace River. He then traveled on a Seminole trail now utilized as a military road to Fort Brooke, passing directly through the ruins of Thonotosassa. I imagine it was a long disheartening trip, viewing the land in which one once prospered now lying in ruins. The military hastened John's departure. On June 14, John was among the thirty Black Seminoles who had reached New Orleans. Accompanying him was one male listed at age 1-10, two males listed age 10-25, one female under ten, two females aged 10-25, and his wife.

John Cavallo was the last significant Black Seminole leader to surrender. Although he was transported out of the Florida Territory in 1838, due to unforeseen events, he would return. Jesup had guaranteed John his freedom but in the West, a claim would be made to the contrary. John's father, Chief Cavallo, died shortly after his arrival in the West. Chief Cavallo's widow insisted that John was her slave by right and not a designated ally to the Seminole Indians. It is most likely she made this claim due to her reliance upon Black Seminoles for agricultural work, especially now that her husband was dead. John now needed formal documentation of his freedom as well as funds for survival. Therefore he agreed to work for the United States military by inducing relatives and friends to emigrate.

In October, Gen. Arbuckle was given authorization to allow John to return to Florida. When Gen. Taylor was notified of John's return he was outraged to say the least. In November, he wrote,

"I regret that permission should have been given for the return to Florida of the Seminole Indian John Co-wia as I believe him to be one of the most artful and faithless of his tribe." Taylor went on to state, "I cannot therefore give my consent to this man's landing in the Territory, and if time allows will take the responsibility to order him to be halted at New Orleans." Taylor never assumed that "responsibility" to prevent John's return. By May 1839, John was back in Florida employed as a military guide and interpreter.

Little is known about John's first year of service as a military guide and interpreter. What is certain is that the job itself was perilous and he was sure to have encountered danger. "Negro guides" became a valued tool to the military. Seminoles also understood the value of the guides to the United States military. In July 1839, a government detachment was ambushed in a camp on the Caloosahatchee River. According to a survivor, "The negro interpreter Sandy [and Sampson] were allowed to live four days. They then tied them to a pine tree and inserted in their flesh slivers of light wood, setting them on fire, and at the same time placing torches at their feet." However, only Sandy was murdered and the other guide, Sampson, was spared due to his relationship with Osceola.

By 1840, John was a well-paid guide of the military. He was known to have visited Black Seminole encampments under military supervision. The Black Seminoles held frequent dances in which John actively participated. It is believed that during a visit to attend a dance John met his wife Susan. It appears that John had two wives, the wife of his youth and Susan. By the spring of 1840, John and Susan were married and remained so for over 40 years until his death. Susan, a Black Seminole herself, was the daughter of July (one of the three former sub-chiefs of Peliklakaha) who, unlike Abraham, remained in Florida as an interpreter. Susan Horse was 19 years old at the time of their wedding. The other wife is never mentioned in relation to John again.

By the summer of 1840, John had gained the trust of Brevet Brig. Gen. Walker K. Armistead. This was primarily due to the fact that John Horse had participated in actual combat against his fellow Seminoles. In the Withlacoochee River region, John accompanied Maj. Beall on an expedition tracking Seminoles in a nearby area. In September, they encountered a Seminole village and were engaged by warriors. Beall directed John to talk to them; while doing so, a Black Seminole informed John that they did not wish to talk and immediately began firing. John returned fire, subsequently fighting his own people. There is no doubt that John was the primary target, given the animosity already expressed towards guides and interpreters for the military. Gen. Armistead, who replaced Taylor as Florida commander, wrote in reference to John,

> Gopher John...who appears honest and intelligent declares that the return of two or three Chiefs from Arkansas...will... [persuade] those now here to emigrate. He states that...the Indians [think] that those shipped for the west were afterwards thrown overboard and if they can be shown that their brethren have not only been spared but well treated, they will be inclined to join them.

Armistead took John's advice. On November 2, Chief Holatoochee, 13 other Seminoles and two interpreters arrived in Tampa. It is almost certain that Holatoochee was chosen on the advice of John. Less than one week later, the delegates contacted the two most prominent Seminole chiefs still fighting in the territory: Chief Halleck Tustenuggee, a Black Seminole; and Tiger Tail, a Tallahassee Seminole Indian. During the negotiations, the two chiefs asked to stay in Florida. If they could not, then they would agree to emigration. Their agreement to emigration appears to have been a negotiation tactic most likely to ensure their safety during negotiations. Once Armistead informed them that he would have to notify his superiors, two weeks later chiefs Tustenuggee and Tiger Tail disappeared, and the war resumed yet again. Holatoochee, on the other hand, continued to bring in Seminoles for emigration. In March 1841, 222 members of the Tallahassee band gathered for emigration and were later shipped out of the Florida Territory. John was well aware of the mistrust of the Seminoles toward Black Seminole guides for the military. He understood that his word would simply not be enough, especially now that most of his comrades had emigrated and he was unfamiliar with the majority of those who were still at war. By bringing in the delegation, John demonstrated his commitment to the Black Seminoles as well as the Seminole Indians, by trying to save as many lives as possible.

In 1841, John Cavallo was the chief interpreter for Col. William J. Worth, who at the time was becoming the leader of the United States' war effort. Worth's efforts at the beginning of 1841 were concentrated on bringing Coacoochee, now the Seminoles' primary chief, in for negotiations and eventual emigration. John, however, was becoming more dissatisfied as he had yet to receive his promise of freedom in writing. In March, Coacoochee met with Worth at Fort Cummings. By utilizing John's influence, Worth was able to reach an emigration agreement with Coacoochee. Shortly afterwards, John would finally receive his freedom in writing, which stated:

> In execution of the promise made by a former commander of the Florida army as certified by his successor, Brigadier General Taylor, the Interpreter John Cohai, commonly called Gopher John, his wife and increase, Indian negroes, having complied with the terms of the foregoing recited order, are regarded as having established a right to their freedom from all further services for their former Indian Master.

John would continue to provide his services to the military until his departure in July 1842. In mid-February, Maj. William G Belknap requested John's presence at his upper Pease Creek camp. Worth obliged him; however, less than a week later he demanded his return. Belknap released both John and Alligator to Worth but sent a message with urgent requests for John's return. He informs

Worth that "the Indians who remain with me...insist on the return." Worth declined, informing Belknap through his aide, "The negro Gopher John cannot be spared...There is much dissatisfaction among some of the Indians [at Fort Brooke], the cause & removal of which can only be affected by the shrewdness & management of John, and the commanding officer regards his presence at this Post of paramount importance." This correspondence demonstrates the trust that the Seminoles still had in John. John, probably more so than Abraham himself, retained the ability throughout the war to effectively maneuver between both sides to garner a satisfactory position for both Seminoles and Black Seminoles alike. John placed himself in whatever position was necessary to accomplish his goal, including fighting on the side of the United States military.

In April 1842, John, in the company of Worth, found himself fighting his fellow Seminoles near Lake Apopka. How did John Cavallo, one of the most outstanding Black Seminole leaders and a formidable foe to the United States, transform into one of the most popular guides and interpreters for the military? Why would he assist the military in any shape, form or fashion? I propose that the answers are much deeper than many imagine. He had a desire to locate family members and, as previously discussed, his freedom in the West was in jeopardy. Nonetheless, it was more than that. John accepted responsibilities for leading Black Seminoles as a matter of duty. His primary goal was to convince his Seminole comrades and fellow Black Seminoles that there was both a life, as well as freedom in the West. To remain in the West as a slave of his father's widow was to accept failure. Like Abraham, he understood the strength of the United States military and the insurmountable odds against the Seminoles. He therefore made a conscious decision that, in the end, securing his and fellow Black Seminoles' freedom justified working with and for the United States military.

Approximately three months after the battle at Lake Apopka, John Cavallo left Florida never to return. Years later, Worth would declare that John had "aided him in getting five hundred and thirty-five Indians." That is to say that John Cavallo secured the life and liberty of 535 Seminoles from the Whites.

John's actions from 1838 to 1842 were a result of his vision for Black Seminoles in the West. Well after emigrating he would continue to have a positive relationship with the United States in order to secure a better life for Black Seminoles in the West. His short stint in the West before his return gave him a glimpse of the upcoming hardships Black Seminoles would have to face. His status as a chief did not shelter him from the possibility of re-enslavement. Therefore, as a leader, he had to have known what would be in store for other Black Seminoles.

In the West, John Cavallo would emerge as John Horse. During the war, he was given the war name Hokepis Hejo or Crazy Beast, an honorary war title meaning his heart is recklessly brave. John was now a seasoned leader who had been tested and proven as both a Seminole leader and war chief through the Second Seminole War. His peers and comrades immediately began to look to his leadership during the tribulations Black Seminoles endured in the West. He would again have to devote himself to securing the freedom of his people. To the Black Seminoles in the West, John Horse was a leader in almost every conceivable manner. He was their politician, ambassador to the United States and Mexican governments, and doctor. Somewhere in his illustrious career, John mastered the art of tribal medicine and provided his people with herbal remedies.

As a result of his leadership, Black Seminoles would receive more security for their freedom in Oklahoma and Texas. He would go on to establish a Black Seminole settlement in Nacimiento, Mexico. In Florida, Abraham was the principal Black Seminole leader and in the West, it would be John Horse. John's life represented a life of leadership and dedication. From his youth, as the son of a chief, he was being prepared to take responsibility for his people. During the war, his charismatic bravery would elevate him from sub-chief to war chief in just a year's time. His role as Alligator's sense bearer and principal adviser would gain him the respect of Seminoles as well as the United States government. His accomplishments during the Second Seminole War as a negotiator, adviser and war commander would provide the necessary skills needed to lead in the West. This in no way belittles his efforts during the war; without John's military strategy and undaunted willingness to wage war, Black Seminoles may very well have been returned to plantation slavery.

Despite seemingly insurmountable odds, Black Seminole leaders were able to wage war and negotiate feasible terms that eventually secured their safety and freedom from plantation society. Their leadership was also responsible for inducing and aiding over 200 slaves to abscond from plantation society. Although their Indian counterparts waged war (for the most part) in order to resist emigration west, these leaders understood that emigration was a feasible alternative for Black Seminoles. In doing so, they further established an autonomy from Seminole Indians which was reflected outside the Seminole Nation. The mere fact that they were able to garner their freedom from plantation society and emigrate west demonstrated a victory against the United States government.

CHAPTER V

THE IMPACT OF BLACK SEMINOLES ON THE SECOND SEMINOLE WAR

When the war ended in August 1842, it had cost the United States over twenty million dollars. This was four times the cost of what the Spanish received for the Florida Territory. In all of the other Indian conflicts from 1866 to 1891, the United States Army lost less than 2,000 men, while the Second Seminole War alone resulted in casualties of more than 1,500 soldiers and sailors, not including the militia. The overall impact of Black Seminoles can be measured by examining their impact on Seminole Indians, plantation society in Florida, and negotiations with and military operations against the United States government.

The nature of the Black–Indian relationship amongst the Seminoles is undoubtedly the essence of their unified front during the war. The dependence of Seminole Indians on Blacks for agricultural production and negotiations with Whites demonstrates the impact of Black Seminoles on Seminole Indians. There is little doubt that this dependence became a factor in the Seminoles' decision to resist the Whites' efforts to divide the two groups.

The exact number of Black Seminoles within the Seminole Nation during the war is unknown. The continuous flow of runaway slaves alone makes an exact calculation virtually impossible. There have been estimates ranging from 300 or 400 to as many as 1,400. The 1834 estimate of more than 500 is considered to be a reasonable guess. This wide range of numbers is perhaps based on the distinction made between runaways and Seminole slaves. Regardless of the ratio of Black Seminoles to Seminole Indians, the impact of Black Seminoles was undeniable. A United States military officer claimed:

> The negroes, from the commencement of the Florida war,
> have, for their numbers, been the most formidable foe, more
> blood-thirsty, active, and revengeful, than the Indian...The

negro, returned to his original owner, might have remained a
few days, when he again would have fled to the swamps, more
vindictive than ever...

For example, regarding the battles in the Withlacoochee region,
United States authorities confirmed that approximately 250 Black
Seminole warriors were active. However, when Gen. Gaines engaged
the Seminoles, the number of Black Seminoles was estimated to be
between four and five hundred. The intensity with which the Black
Seminoles fought is one of the likely causes of the disparity in the
numbers reported in the sources. It would be difficult to say that
the intensity of the Black Seminole warriors did not impact their
Indian counterparts.

The Black Seminoles' fighting intensity appealed to the more
militant Indian leaders. Osceola became their most trusted ally not
for sentimental reasons, but because of his vigorous opposition to
re-enslavement. His rise in the Seminole Nation as a war chief was
based upon his charisma and merits. He had no hereditary claim to
the chieftaincy. His band primarily consisted of those who respected
his militancy, courage and intelligence, many of whom were Black.
During the war, Osceola would synchronize his movements with
Black Seminole leaders.

According to Gen. Jesup, the loss of Blacks would weaken
the Indians "more than they would be weakened by the loss of
the same number of their own people." The influence of Black
Seminoles during negotiations as well as the intensity with which
they fought certainly bolsters Jesup's assertion. The lack of the
Black Seminole leaders' support after 1838 and the large reduction
of Black Seminole involvement as a result of their agreement to
emigrate influenced the Seminole Indian war effort until 1842.
Certainly, the loss of Seminole Indian leaders and warriors affected
their decisions more so than the withdrawal of Black Seminoles.
However, it cannot be said that the increasing scarcity of their Black
allies had no relevance to the Indians at all. The Black Seminoles

had successfully convinced the Seminole Indians that their fates were linked. It is my contention that because their fates were intertwined in the minds of both Black and Indian leadership, the primary motive behind their struggle was to ensure that Blacks and Indians would continue to live together free of White control, interference and bondage.

The evidence that supports this assertion is the general agreement of Indians to the Articles of Capitulation after the inclusion of Article V. Once Jesup agreed to allow the Black Seminoles to emigrate with their Indian counterparts, a large number of Indians began to assemble for emigration. Furthermore, once the slaveholders disrupted the process, both Indians and Blacks alike refused to emigrate. Jesup notified one of his lieutenants that the claims of Black Seminole ownership by Whites would cause Indian removal to "be greatly delayed, if not entirely prevented." This demonstrates to a large degree that at this point (1837), the desire to stay together was more important or as important to Indians as their desire to remain in Florida.

The fact that the Black Seminoles had a significant impact on the plantation society in Florida is beyond question. More slaves in Florida were reported absent from their masters during the Second Seminole War than in the 13 years prior to 1835. Between 1821 and 1834, 159 slaves were reported as runaways, while 185 were reported during the war. The year 1838, (the year after the inclusion of Article V in the Articles of Capitulation), witnessed the second-largest number of reported runaway slaves over a span of 49 years.

Slave violence manifested itself through stealing and the destruction of property and human lives. The plantation raids, primarily under the leadership and direction of John Caesar, demonstrated the Black Seminoles' influence upon slave resistance. Black Seminoles exhorted slaves to seize their freedom by relieving themselves of their masters, advice which certainly did not fall on deaf ears. The fact that most individual acts of violence perpetrated against Whites were premeditated indicates a degree of planning and perhaps forethought regarding the possibility of escaping punishment.

It is therefore likely that even if the exhortations by Black Seminoles were not a primary factor that motivated a particular act of violence, the promise of a safe haven after an escape certainly made resistance a more viable option for some slaves. It is also important to note that the impact of slave violence extended beyond Florida's borders. In 1837, Gen. Thomas S. Jesup reported, "seven runaways from Georgia...well armed and plenty of ammunition... have left and on their way south [and] burned the houses in the vicinity." Slaves who took part in the Stono Rebellion of South Carolina headed for the Edisto River. This river opens up directly north of St. Augustine, presumably their goal.

Whites were never oblivious to the growing relationship among Blacks. Their concerns over slave violence were not taken lightly to say the least. In 1824, a statute was enacted, declaring:

> Be it further enacted that if any slave shall consult, advise, or conspire to rebel, or make insurrection against the white inhabitants of this [Florida] territory, or against the laws of the government thereof, or shall plot or conspire the murder of any white person, or shall commit an assault and battery, on any white person with an intention to kill, he or she shall, on conviction of either of the said crimes, suffer death.

As tensions mounted between the Seminole Nation and Whites, their concerns over a Black alliance quickly developed into apprehension. Whites responded with a demand for harsher slave codes and further movement restrictions. Prior to the outbreak of war, Gen. Duncan Clinch expressed the sentiment that "if a sufficient military force...is not sent...the whole frontier may be laid waste by a combination of the Indians, Indian Negroes, and the Negroes on the plantations." Later he would report, "Some of the most respectable planters fear that there is already a secret and improper communication carried on between the refractory Indians, Indian Negroes, and some of the plantation Negroes."

Free Blacks were also watched with careful and suspicious eyes. During the height of the war, virtually any non-combatant contact between free Blacks and Black Seminoles could result in charges of treason for free Blacks. A Florida bill was passed stipulating that any free Black caught aiding the Seminole cause was to be sold into slavery. In 1836, Major Benjamin A Putnam of the Florida militia strongly suggested to Governor Call a standing court-martial to deal with Blacks in violation of the law.

Once Black resistance escalated within plantation society, primarily in the form of plantation raids, apprehensions quickly turned into fear. Those planters who did survive the raids of 1835 began to move into towns such as St. Augustine, Jacksonville and Pensacola for safety, leaving their plantations, farms and small settlements abandoned. As a result, plantation society's growth, particularly in the St. Johns River region, was curbed during the first years of the war. The violence perpetrated upon plantations also caused a change in the production of work and work habits. Louis Goldsborough, an overseer in 1835 admitted, "neither our Negroes nor others can work with the same heart of life they [do] otherwise."

A few years later, the ensuing threat of raids would cause this same overseer to declare that "if Osceola [and his band of Black Seminoles] came, and I find myself forced to abandon Wirt land to his mercy…I shall take all the Negroes to Pensacola." It was not long before the United States government came to the realization that they were not going to simply persuade the Seminole Indians into selling Blacks to them. In fact, the ultimate decision to remove the Seminole Indians was deemed the only solution to ridding Florida of the Black communities outside of White control. This decision was made only after attempts to gain Blacks from the Indians had failed. It appears that the Whites' desire for cheap slaves was the driving force behind the separation of the Seminole Nation.

The impact of Black Seminoles on United States policy concerning negotiations with the Seminole Indians before the war officially began is duly noted in the treaties of Payne's Landing and Indian Springs. As the Second Seminole War drew closer, White dissatisfaction with the Black–Indian alliance manifested itself in almost every policy concerning the Seminole Indians. In 1832, to exert more control over trade with the Seminoles and eventually force emigration, territory officials prohibited bond or free Indian Negroes from leaving Seminole lands. In 1834, Governor DuVal and Indian agent Wiley Thompson advised the War Department that "The Negroes are more provident than the Indians. They not only often feed the hungry Indian but having the means they introduce by stealth into the nation sometimes considerable quantities of whiskey...to gratify the vitiated and intemperate appetite of the Indian." That same year, DuVal further went on to advise the Commissioner of Indian Affairs that the first step to relocating the Seminoles west "must be the breaking up of the runaways slaves and outlaw Indians." Once the war began, the Black Seminoles' impact on the United States military would affect both its policies and strategies.

The failure of the United States to defeat the Seminoles in the first year of the war was evident by mid-1836. The War Department's order to Gen. Scott to remove the Seminoles while offering no peace as long as the Blacks were with them was simply unenforceable. When Gen. Jesup replaced Scott by the end of the year, it took less than a month's time for him to understand the impact and importance of the Black Seminoles. On December 9, 1836, Jesup reported, "This, you may be assured, [the Second Seminole War] is a Negro, not an Indian war." In March, he would write, "The Negroes...rule the Indians...if they should...hold out, the war will be renewed." Jesup would, from this point until the end of his tenure as commander in 1838, develop policies based on this belief because he did not understand that above all (for both sides) slavery was the main issue.

Jesup's declaration of the Seminole War being a Negro War would not be accepted by the United States until 1841, when it officially abandoned the idea of recapturing all Black Seminoles and removing the remaining Blacks in custody, as well as those captured through the end of the war in 1842, to the West with their Indian counterparts. This policy, which basically voided the Indian Springs Treaty, was expressed by Colonel William Worth. In a letter dated August 19, 1841, Worth wrote, "Indians have been solemnly guaranteed retention of slaves indifferently...to the mode or time... they obtained possession."

Jesup's declaration, for the purpose of this study, is pertinent to the claim that the war was indeed a slave rebellion. The policy adopted in 1841 revealed the willingness of the United States military to embrace this idea. The first act was the military's policy of utilizing Black Seminole leaders to assure both Blacks and Indians that their safe passage to the West was guaranteed. It has been noted that this policy was not to all the Whites' liking, but nevertheless effective.

Sources claiming that Negroes ruled Seminole Indians, had controlling influence and somewhat governed them suggest the belief of Whites that the Seminole Nation was highly influenced by its Black members. The presence of Black Seminoles within the Seminole Nation was a major cause of the war itself. The Seminole Indians may have been allowed to remain in some portion of Florida initially had it not been for the presence of Blacks in their communities. The decision to remove the Black Seminoles from the Seminole Nation preceded the one for the removal of the Seminole Indians from the territory. The ever-increasing persistence of Whites to place Blacks in servitude within their society was not only the primary aim, but the sole reason for the continuation of the war. Thus, when the Second Seminole War is re-conceptualized under these circumstances and premises, the conflict must be re-examined in light of its resemblance to a massive slave rebellion against pro-slavery interests.

The Black Seminole Maroon society, like all Black Maroon societies, often fought against Whites in a struggle for survival. Past comparisons of Black Seminoles to Jamaican and Suriname Maroons reveal each group's efforts to retain African cultural traditions, to negotiate with European powers and to establish relationships with slaves. The key feature that separates the Black Seminoles from most Maroon societies is that while the Jamaican and Suriname Maroons existed almost solely on their own by negotiating and coming to terms with various Whites over a period of time, the Black Seminoles were able to maintain a constant Indian ally. This afforded them the opportunity to resist the threat of enslavement and removal, unlike their counterparts in Jamaica and Suriname.

Ten conditions have been identified as favorable or conducive for a slave rebellion. Of these, six existed in Florida during this period:

1. Geographical conditions favored guerilla warfare.

2. Dominance of a large-scale monopolistic enterprise. The three primary regions of the Florida territory each were dominated by a primary crop.

3. Low ratio of local slaves to foreign-born slaves. Although technically this was not the case, the fact that the Black Seminoles formed a separate culture of their own, those runaways that joined them were outsiders until they were acculturated into the society. Thus the "local" slaves would be the recent runaways in comparison to the Black Seminoles.

4. The imported slaves, or a significant portion of them, were of common ethnic origin. Here, Black Seminoles would be considered those of a "common ethnic origin." The fact that the Black Seminoles created a different culture from those

of recent runaways does not detract from the principle of ethnic commonality.

5. The social structure of the slave-holding regime permitted the emergence of an autonomous Black leadership.

6. The formation of colonies of runaway slaves strong enough to threaten the plantation regime was provided by the geographical, social and political environment.

Once the war is conceptualized as a slave rebellion, comparisons to other known conspiracies and rebellions help to place this research in a larger context. The 1811 rebellion in southern Louisiana is considered the largest rebellion on North American soil. It is estimated that 180 slaves armed with axes, weapons and a small number of firearms marched towards New Orleans. They were repelled and the rebellion was put down by the collective efforts of slaveholders, a free Black militia, and federal troops. The rebellion was largely directed towards the destruction of plantations. Only a small number of Whites were killed. In the end, 66 slaves were murdered, while 16 of their leaders were executed. The number of slave participants indicates the main justification for declaring this rebellion as the largest. If this is indeed the case, then the Second Seminole War should actually be considered the largest slave rebellion on American soil. When compared to the Louisiana rebellion, the war involved three times as many Black participants.

The Nat Turner Rebellion is considered the deadliest slave rebellion in North America. As a result of this rebellion, approximately 55 Whites were murdered, including men, women and children. The shock resulting from the number of Whites killed propelled the impact of the rebellion far beyond Southampton County, Virginia. In comparison, the number of Whites murdered in Virginia represents a small fraction of the number of White soldiers, militia men, and members of plantation society killed during the war in Florida, which numbers over 1,000. This ultimately means that the war was also the deadliest slave rebellion.

The major slave conspiracies or rebellions in the United States were linked to larger revolutions or conflicts that involved freedom and equality. Both the Gabriel Prosser conspiracy of 1800 and the Denmark Vesey conspiracy of 1822 were inspired by the belief that broader conflicts of the period would bolster the rebellion's chances of success. For example, an undeclared war between the United States and France, along with French revolutionary ideology, made Prosser confident that the French would help his cause. Unfortunately, both the Prosser and Vesey conspiracies would never develop into rebellion. Nat Turner was partially inspired to instigate rebellion shortly after a Virginia Constitutional convention sided with the slave owners over issues within. Black Seminoles were no different in taking cues from public discourse about liberty. They immediately began to incorporate themselves within the Seminole removal debate once it appeared to offer them better protection against (re-)enslavement.

The similarities between Prosser, Vesey, Turner and Abraham reveal prerequisites for leadership among rebellious slaves. All of these men had some mastery of the English language. Prosser, Vesey and Turner were able to both read and write, while Abraham was able to translate English into the Seminole language. They also all received privileges due to their special talents. Prosser, a skilled blacksmith; Turner, a Christian minister; and Abraham, a chief counselor, were able to attract more followers by being in an elevated position and having more freedom to travel and meet potential allies. Denmark Vesey and Abraham were able to gain their freedom as a result of their special talents. The average field-hand slave who had limited contact with those outside of their plantation was far less likely to acquire a large following. These particular men were leaders among their respective Black communities before they embarked upon rebellions.

These rebel leaders understood the importance of religion and spirituality to their respective Black communities. They were able to incorporate these appeals as a way to justify the act of rebellion. When necessary, they would stress Christian doctrine or African spiritual exhortations to their followers. For Prosser and Turner, Christian ideology was primarily utilized, while Abraham relied on a more African-centered spirituality. Vesey utilized radical Christian doctrine in his attempts to garner support, while at the same time employing Jack Pritchard, an African mystic, to influence slaves who were not Christian. Thus, Vesey utilized a combination of Christian- and African-centered doctrines. Regardless of the leader, the African influence of "conjuring" appears to be a distinctive influence in all four cases.

The similarities between the Black Seminoles during the Second Seminole War and three of the largest slave conspiracies and rebellions highlight obvious characteristics of collective slave resistance. The impact of the Black Seminoles on the Florida Territory suggests that the issue of slavery was not only as important as the removal of Seminole Indians but, at crucial points during the conflict, more important. The circumstances that were both surrounding and intrinsic to the development of war highlight several pre-existing conditions necessary for a rebellion. The involvement, leadership and impact of the Black Seminoles caused the Second Seminole War to become a situational or opportunistic slave rebellion. Furthermore, it was the largest, longest, deadliest and, by far, the most successful slave rebellion in the United States.

OVERVIEW AND CONCLUSION

Beginning in the 17th century, the Spanish sought to control Florida in order to maintain a foothold in the New World. Free Blacks formed militias as early as 1683 and agreed to help defend St. Augustine from outside European invasion in exchange for certain liberties. The Spanish provided food until the first crops were harvested, a priest for religious instruction and established a military presence at Fort Mose. Spanish officials also encouraged both runaway slaves and Native Americans from nearby English colonies to settle in Florida. As early as 1739, fugitive slaves were settling in and around Fort Mose. Although a precise date as to when other free Blacks, runaway slaves, Black slaves owned by Seminole Indians, and the Seminole Indians formed a bond is not known, 1763, the year Florida was ceded to the English, is the year they became a recognized community by those outside the area.

As a result of the decrease in the number of Spaniards in Florida, Seminoles began to acquire more Blacks from European settlers (both Spanish and English). The Seminoles, unlike their English counterparts in the area, were not interested in the complete control of Black lives. Also, because the Seminoles did not have the same pressing needs for agriculture, the work requirements on Blacks were vastly different.

Over a period of time, Blacks began to prosper and increase in numbers. They either lived in separate communities, establishing their own towns and villages near Seminole Indians, or joined Indians by cohabitating or intermarriage. Through this cohabitation, Blacks became an integral part of Seminole society, assuming positions as trusted interpreters to the English, advisers and counselors. Thus, they became known as the Black Seminoles. By taking these positions, they were afforded the opportunity to identify themselves as Blacks in the company of, but not the same as, Seminole Indians.

African retentions appear to have been a driving force in the perceptions of the Black Seminoles. Because they were allowed to form their own identity and culture, Black Seminoles were able to retain a strong tie to African cultures. In their case, as with most Maroon societies, freedom was not only an escape from enslavement, but also a chance to continue their own African-inspired way of life in a manner of their own choosing with minimal outside interference. By incorporating Spanish, Indian, English and American plantation cultures into their own African culture, Black Seminoles were able to produce an identity much to their own choosing. This is not to say that they were not deeply influenced by these outside cultures; however, these influences did not completely overwhelm their African-derived sensibilities.

The relationship between Seminole Blacks and Indians began with a basic empathy for one another. They both understood each other's desire to maintain their freedom and a life of their own choosing. The intermarriage and cultural exchange between the two resulted in a durable relationship. That bond was strengthened through the codependency that developed. White settlers' resentment and ill sentiments towards their alliance also strengthened their bond, in that if the Black Seminoles and Seminole Indians had nothing else in common, they at least had a common foe.

For those Blacks who were slaves to Seminole Indians, their relationship resembled more of a landlord/client relationship. Generally, the term "slave" became more of a negotiating reference with Whites. By the 1820s, the Black Seminoles were down to their last and most trusted ally, the Seminole Indians. Up to this point, Blacks were able to maintain their existence through alliances with Spanish and British authorities in exchange for their military contributions protecting the respective European interests in the Florida Territory. However, by 1821, both the British and Spanish governments had relinquished their claims to Florida. The Seminole

Indians had also come to rely on their military contributions. Thus, by the end of the decade when the United States ordered the removal of the Seminoles west of the Mississippi River, Blacks would again be called upon for military service.

The Black Seminoles knew that their plight was tied to that of the Seminoles. Prior treaties between Indians and the United States basically eliminated all claims by the Seminole Indians on Black Seminoles and made Blacks susceptible to slave-catching expeditions. It was clear that the United States intended to destroy Black Seminole society and enslave Blacks on White plantations. In fact, the decision to move the Seminole Indians westward was based upon, to a large degree, the need to separate Indians from Blacks. Their separation would cause Black Seminoles to become vulnerable to capture and enslavement.

During the first three years of the war, Black Seminole warriors were highly visible during combat. They participated in every major battle during this period. Their destruction of plantations in remote areas caused panic along the Florida frontier. Their intimate knowledge of the Florida wilderness enhanced their ability to successfully execute guerilla tactics against the United States military. The success of the Seminoles' military efforts heavily relied upon the success of these guerilla tactics. Black Seminole warriors were regarded as the fiercest opponents of the US military during the war.

The Black Seminoles' struggle for freedom played as much a role in the development of their society as anything else. Their military strength allowed them to forge alliances, increase their numbers and sustain their way of life. It defined their society in a way that distinguished them from Indians. Unlike their enslaved counterparts on the plantations, they did not wait for particular incidents to incite them to violence. Politically, the Black Seminole leaders' participation in negotiations as translators and counselors afforded them the ability to become more vital members of the Seminole Nation, while pursuing the interests of their own communities. Their active roles during negotiations also created a dependency on the part of both Whites and Indians alike. Once this dependency was created, Black Seminole leaders began to execute plans different from the objectives of Seminole Indians during the war. As Seminole Indians were still fighting against removal from 1838 to 1842, Black Seminole leaders were actively working with the United States military to secure their people's safe passage westward.

Black Seminole leaders also actively led bands of warriors that consisted of both Blacks and Indians. They became known as war chiefs due to their military fortitude and prowess in combat. Each of the three primary Black Seminole leaders brought a new dimension to the war that only a Black Seminole could. Abraham, the primary Black Seminole leader during the war, eloquently negotiated favorable terms for Blacks that allowed them to emigrate westward. By recognizing the dependency of both Whites and Indians, he was able to garner support from both sides in his endeavor to secure Black Seminoles their freedom. John Caesar wreaked havoc on the White community of East Florida by destroying plantations during the first year and a half of the war. He was also the primary intermediary and instigator of plantation slaves. His actions alone increased the likelihood of a mass slave insurrection within Florida more than any other single development during the war. John Cavallo's character and high position within the Seminole Nation allowed him the opportunity to ensure the freedom of more Blacks than any other person. From 1838 to 1842, John Cavallo was responsible for securing the safe passage of approximately 500 Blacks and Indians to the West.

It would not take Whites long to understand that the actual number of Black Seminole participants certainly in no way reflected their importance or impact during the war. Their influence on the disruption, damage and destruction of plantation society increased White Floridians' fear and apprehension. Black Seminoles' heavy influence on both plantation slaves and Indians alike caused Whites to believe that the Black Seminoles' presence was the most pressing obstacle to attaining their goals. Whites quickly realized that the most formidable foe they faced in their efforts to enslave the Black Seminoles was the Black Seminoles themselves and not the Indians. They would go on to declare the Second Seminole War a war with Blacks.

Black Seminoles' participation during the war would cause the United States to redirect its military operations, institute a separate policy concerning Black Seminoles and, ultimately, abandon their objective to place Black Seminoles within their society as slaves. Black Seminole villages became the targets of the United States military after several embarrassing conflicts. There was simply no conceivable way to explain to the rest of the country, and especially to those in Washington, how a force so small could resist their military might. Despite the arrogance of Whites in their beliefs of racial superiority, the military was forced into diplomacy with a race of people they had little regard for as human beings. In 1841, when the United States officially abandoned their efforts to reduce Black Seminoles to slavery and allowed them to emigrate westward, it was tantamount to accepting defeat.

By re-examining the Second Seminole War from the Black Seminole perspective, this book frames the war primarily as a slave rebellion and not as an Indian war. There is no question as to the validity of the belief that Black Seminole society in Florida was a Maroon society. However, when examining the context of the United States government's actions from 1821 to 1842 concerning the Black Seminoles, a unique case develops unlike the situation of other Maroon societies. What this study has demonstrated is that during this period a Maroon society exploded into a mass rebellion. The fact that there were more Seminole Indian participants does not overshadow the essence of the war.

Attitudes which belittled the Black Seminole involvement in

the war in 19th-century writings are still reflected in the latest historiographies concerning the Second Seminole War. Although the issue of slavery has been ably dealt with by scholars in recent years, those who were most affected by the issue have not. Black Seminoles, for the most part, are still being relegated to the position of Blacks in the company of Indians. Names such as Micanopy, Wild Cat and Osceola have become synonymous with the war, while names such as Abraham, John Caesar and John Cavallo are at best secondarily considered. We must continue to challenge this particular characterization of the historical record and shed more light on the significance of the Black Seminole experience in Floridian as well as American history. Moreover, we must continue to conduct research and examine major events from the Black perspective. This in turn will help eradicate the continued relegation of the African-American contributions and their experiences as simply "Blacks in the company of…"

SOURCES

Firsthand/Primary Sources: Documents, Manuscripts and Collections

Acts and Resolutions of the Legislative Council of the Territory of Florida, 1822–1845. State Library of Florida, Tallahassee.

William W Belknap. Papers. Xerographic copy in the collection of the author. State Library of Florida, Tallahassee.

Robert J Bigelow. Papers. PK Yonge Library of Florida History, University of Florida, Gainesville.

Florida Territorial Papers. State Library of Florida, Tallahassee.

Louis Goldsborough. Papers. Library of Congress, Washington, DC.

Ethan A Hitchcock. Papers. Xerographic copy in the collection of the author. National Archives, Southeast Branch, Morrow.

Nathan S Jarvis. Diary. PK Yonge Library of Florida History, University of Florida, Gainesville.

Thomas S. Jesup. Diary. Xerographic copy in the collection of the author. State Library of Florida, Tallahassee.

Thomas S. Jesup. Papers. State Library of Florida, Tallahassee.

John B Stetson. Collection. PK Yonge Library of Florida History, University of Florida, Gainesville.

WJ. Worth. Papers. Xerographic copy in the collection of the author. State Library of Florida, Tallahassee.

Firsthand/Primary Sources: Government Documents

American State Papers, Indian Affairs. National Archives, Southeast Branch, Morrow.

American State Papers, Military Affairs. National Archives, Southeast Branch, Morrow.

Congressional Globe. HB Wells Library, Indiana University, Bloomington.

Department of Indian Affairs. National Archives, Southeast Branch, Morrow.

United States Congressional Papers. National Archives, Southeast Branch, Morrow.

United States State and Territorial Papers. National Archives, Southeast Branch, Morrow.

United States War Department, Adjutant General's Office. National Archives, Southeast Branch, Morrow.

Firsthand/Primary Sources: Newspapers and Periodicals

Apalachicola Courier

Apalachicola Gazette

Army and Navy Chronicle

Charleston (SC) Courier

Fernandina East Floridian

Jacksonville Courier

Key West Enquirer

Niles' Weekly Register

St. Augustine East Florida Advocate

St. Augustine Florida Herald

St. Augustine News

Tallahassee Florida Watchman

Tampa Florida Peninsular

Tampa Sunday Tribune

Secondhand/Secondary Sources: Theses and Dissertations

Boyett, Cheryll. "The Seminole Black Alliance during the Second Seminole War 1835–1842," MA Thesis, California State University, Dominquez Hill, Ann Arbor, 1997.

Hall, Robert L. "Do, Lord, Remember Me: Religion, and Cultural Charge among Blacks in Florida, 1565–1906," PhD Dissertation, Florida State University, 1984.

Harris, Donorena. "Abolitionist Sentiment in Florida, 1821–1860," MA Thesis, Florida State University, 1989.

Klos, George. "Black Seminoles in Territorial Florida," MA Thesis, Florida State University, 1990.

Micco, Melinda B. "Freedmen and Seminoles: Forging a Seminole Nation," PhD Dissertation, University of California, Berkeley, 1995.

Rivers, Larry E. "Florida's Dissenters, Rebels, and Runaways: Territorial Days to Emancipation," PhD Dissertation, University of London, 2001.

Weik, Terrance Maurice. "A Historical Archaeology of Black Seminole Maroons in Florida: Ethnogenesis and Culture Contact at Pilakaha," PhD Dissertation, University of Florida, 2002.

White, John C. Jr. "American Military Strategy in the Second Seminole War." MS Thesis, Marine Corps Command and Staff College, 1995.

Secondhand/Secondary Sources: Books

Apetheker, Herbert. American Negro Slave Revolts. New York: International Publishers, 1974.

Bell, John H. Letter from John H Bell, Acting Agent for the Indians in Florida to the Hon. John Floyd, of the House of Representatives of the US Relative to Indian Settlements in Florida. Washington, DC.: Gales and Seaton, 1822.

Bembrose, John, edited by Mahon, John K. Reminiscences of the Second Seminole War. Gainesville: University of Florida Press, 1966.

Berlin, Ira. Many Thousands Gone. Cambridge: Belknap Press of Harvard University Press, second printing by the President and Fellows of Harvard College, 1998.

Brown, Canter. Florida's Peace River Frontier. Orlando: University of Central Florida Press, 1991.

Buker, George E. Swamp Sailors: River Warfare in the Everglades 1835–1842. Gainesville: University of Florida Press, 1975.

Carter, Clarence E. (ed.) Territorial Papers of the United States. New York: AMS Publishing, 1973.

Cline, Howard F. Notes on Colonial Indians and Communities in Florida, 1700–1821. New York: Garland Publishing Inc., 1974.

Coe, Charles H. Red Patriots: the story of the Seminoles. Gainesville: University Presses of Florida, 1898 reprint 1974.

Cohen, Meyer M. Notices of Florida and the Campaigns. Gainesville: University of Florida Press, 1836 reprint 1964.

Cusick, James. The Other War of 1812: the Patriot War and the American Invasion of Spanish East Florida. Gainesville: University of Florida Press, 2003.

Deagan, Kathleen, Fort Mose: Colonial America's Black Fortress of Freedom. Gainesville: University Press of Florida, Florida Museum of Natural History, 1995.

Edgerton, Douglass. Gabriel's Rebellion. Chapel Hill: University of North Carolina Press, 1993.

Foreman, Grant. Indian Removal: The Emigration of Five Civilized Tribes of Indians. Norman: University of Oklahoma, 1932.

Franklin, John H., Schweninger, Loren. Runaway Slaves: Rebels on the Plantation. New York: Oxford University Press, 1999.

Fredrickson, George. The Black Image in the White Mind: The Debate on Afro-American Character and Destiny, 1817–1914. Hanover: Wesleyan University Press, 1987.

Gannon, Michale (ed.) The New History of Florida. Gainesville: University Press of Florida, 1996.

Genovese, Eugene. From Rebellion to Revolution: Afro-American Slave Revolts in the Making of the New World. New York: Vintage Books, 1979.

Giddings, Joshua. The Exiles of Florida. Gainesville: University of Florida Press, 1964.

Guinn, Jeff. Our Land Before We Die: The Proud Story of The Seminole Negro. New York: Penguin Putnam, 2002.

Hancock, I. The Texas Seminole and Their Language. Austin: African and Afro-American Studies & Research Center, The University of Texas at Austin, 1980.

Heidler, David S. The War of 1812. Westport: Greenwood Press, 2002.

Hitchcock, Ethan A. Fifty Years in Camp and Field, Diary of Major-General Ethan Allen Hitchcock, USA. New York: GP Putnam's Sons, 1909.

Jay, John, Johnson, Henry P. (ed.) The Correspondence and Public Papers of John Jay, 1782–1793, Volume 3. New York: JP Putnam and Sons, 1891.

Jordan, Winthrop D. Tumult and Silence at Second Creek. Baton Rouge: Louisiana State University Press, 1995.

_____. White Over Black: American Attitudes Toward the Negro, 1550–1812. New York: WW Norton, 1968.

Kappler, Charles J. (ed.) Indian Affairs: Laws and Treaties. Washington, DC.: US Department of the Interior, 1979.

Knetsch, Joe. Florida's Seminole Wars 1817–1858. Charleston: Arcadia Publishing, 2003.

Landers, Jane. Black Society in Spanish Florida. Urbana: University of Chicago Press, 1999.

Laumer, Frank. Massacre. Gainesville: University of Florida Press, 1968.

Levine, Lawrence. Black Culture and Black Consciousness: Afro-American Folk Thought from Slavery to Freedom. New York: Oxford UP, 1977.

Littlefield, Daniel. Africans and Seminoles. Westport: Greenwood Press, 1977.

Mahon, John K. History of the Second Seminole War, 1835–1842 Gainesville: University of Florida Press, 1985.

McCall, George A. Letters from the Frontier. Gainesville: University of Florida Press, 1974.

McKay, Donald B. Pioneer Florida. Tampa: Southern Publication Company, 1959.

Missell, John and Missell, Mary Lou. The Seminole Wars: America's Longest Indian Conflict. Gainesville: University Press of Florida, 2004.

Morgan, Phillip D. Slave Counterpoint. Chapel Hill: University of North Carolina Press, 1998.

Morse, Jedidah. A report to the Secretary of War of the United States on Indian Affairs, Comprising a narrative of a tour performed in the summer of 1820, under a commission from the President of the United States for the purpose of ascertaining for the use of the government, the actual state of the Indian tribes in our Country. St Clair Shores: Scholarly Press, c. 1822, 1972 reprint.

Mulroy, Kevin. Freedom on the Border. Lubbock: Texas Tech University Press, 1993.

Oates, Stephen B. The Fires of Jubilee: Nat Turner's Fierce Rebellion. New York: New American Library, 1975.

Oatis, Steven J. A Colonial Complex: South Carolina's Frontiers in the Era of the Yamasee War, 1680–1730. Lincoln: University of Nebraska Press, 2004.

O'Brien, Sean M. In bitterness and in tears: Andrew Jackson's destruction of the Creeks and Seminoles. Westport: Praeger Publishing, 2003.

Peters, Virginia B. Florida Wars. Hamden: Archon Books, 1995.

Poinsett, Joel R. Report from Secretary of War. Washington, DC.: Government Printing Office, 1838.

Porter, Kenneth W. The Black Seminoles: History of a Freedom Seeking People. Gainesville: University of Florida Press, 1996.

Price, Richard, (ed.) Maroon Societies: Rebel Slave Communities in the Americas. Baltimore: Johns Hopkins UP, 1979.

Prince, Henry. Amidst a Storm of Bullets: The Diary of Lt Henry Prince in Florida, 1836–1842, Ed. Frank Laumer. Tampa: University of Tampa Press, 1998.

Rivers, Larry E. Slavery in Florida. Gainesville: University Press of Florida, 2000.

Robertson, David. Denmark Vesey. New York: Alfred A Knopf, 1999.

Schwalm, Leslie. Hard Fight For We: Women's Transition from Slavery to Freedom in South Carolina. Urbana: University of Illinois Press, 1997.

Segal, Ronald. The Black Diaspora. New York: Noonday Press, 1996.

Simmons, W.H. Notices of East Florida with an account of the Seminole Nation of Indians. Gainesville: University of Florida Press, 1822; reprint 1973.

Smith, Julia. Slavery & Plantation Growth in Antebellum Florida. Gainesville: University of Florida Press, 1973.

Sprague, John T. Origin, Progress, and Conclusion of the Florida War. New York: D. Appleton and Company, 1848.

Stuckey, Sterling. Slave Culture: Nationalist Theory & the Foundations of Black America. New York: Oxford UP, 1987.

Tebeau, Charlton W. A History of Florida. Coral Gables: University of Miami Press, 1971.

The Territorial Papers of the United States. Washington, DC.: US Government Printing Office, 1934.

Turner, Lorenzo. Africanisms in the Gullah Dialect. Chicago: University of Chicago Press, 1949.

Twyman, Bruce E. The Black Seminole Legacy and North American Politics, 1693-1845. Washington, DC.: Howard University Press, 1999.

Wait, T.B. and Sons, (ed.) State and Publick Documents of the United States, from the accession of George Washington to the presidency, exhibiting a complete view of our foreign relations since that time. Volume 9. Boston: Thomas B. Wait and Sons, 1819.

Walton, George. Fearless and Free: The Seminole Indian War, 1835-1842. Indianapolis: Bobbs-Merrill Company, Inc., 1977.

Weisman, Brent R. Like Beads on a String: A Culture History of the Seminole Indians in North Peninsular Florida. Tuscaloosa: University of Alabama Press, 1989.

Wood, Peter. Black Majority: Negroes in Colonial South Carolina from 1670 through the Stono Rebellion. New York: WW Knopf, 1974.

Secondhand/Secondary Sources: Articles

Adams, George R. "The Caloosahatchee Massacre: Its Significance in the Second Seminole War," Florida Historical Quarterly 48.4 (April, 1970): 366-380.

Allen, Paul. "Subduing the Seminoles." Military Historical Quarterly 12.3 (2000): 54-63.

Anderson, Robert L. "The End of an Idyll." Florida Historical Quarterly 42.2 (1967): 35-48.

Batemen, Rebecca B. "Naming Patterns in Black Seminole Ethnogenesis." Ethnohistory 49.2 (2002): 227-257.

_____. "Africans and Indians: A Comparative Study of the Black Carib and Black Seminole." Ethnohistory 37.1 (1990): 1-24.

Bittle, George C. "First Campaign of the Second Seminole War." Florida Historical Quarterly 46.1 (July, 1967): 39-45.

_____. "The Florida Militia's Role in the Battle of Withlacoochee." Florida Historical Quarterly 44.4 (April, 1966): 303-312.

Brown, Canter Jr. "Persifor F. Smith, the Louisiana Volunteers, and the Second Seminole War." Louisiana History 34.4 (1993): 389-410.

_____. "Race Relations in Territorial Florida: 1812–1845." Florida Historical Quarterly 73.3 (January, 1995): 287-308.

_____. "Tales of Angola: Free Blacks, Red Stick Creeks, and International Intrigue In Spanish Southwest Florida, 1812–1821" in Jackson, David H. and Brown, Canter Brown, Eds. Go Sound the Trumpet! Tampa: University of Tampa Press, 2005: 5-21.

_____. "The Florida Crisis of 1826–1827 and the Second Seminole War," Florida Historical Quarterly 73.4 (April, 1995): 420-422.

_____. "The Sarrazota, or Runaway Negro Plantations: Tampa Bay's First Black Community, 1812–1821." Tampa Bay History 12 (Fall/Winter, 1990): 5-19.

Braund, Kathryn E. H. "The Creek Indians, Blacks, and Slavery." Journal of Southern History 57.4 (November, 1991): 601-636.

Brown, Walton L. "The Forgotten Heritage: African-Amerindian Relations in America." Proteus 9.1 (1992): 11-17.

Boyd, Mark F. "Asi-Ya Hola or Osceola." Florida Historical Quarterly 32.3-4 (January-April, 1955): 249-270.

_____. "Events at Prospect Bluff on the Apalachicola River, 1808–1818." Florida Historical Quarterly 16.2 (October, 1937): 55-96.

_____. "Florida Aflame: The Seminole War, Its Background and Onset." Florida Historical Quarterly 30.1 (July, 1951): 1-115.

_____. "Horatio Dexter and the Events Leading to the Treaty of Moultrie Creek with the Seminole Indians." Florida Anthropologist 11: 65-95.

Chandler, Captain William. "An Alarm at Tallahassee, 1836." Florida Historical Quarterly 8.4 (April, 1930): 197-200.

Coker, Edward C. and Schafer, Daniel L., Eds. "A West Point Graduate in the Second Seminole War: William Warren Chapman and the View from Fort Foster," Florida Historical Quarterly 68.4 (April, 1990): 447-475.

Covington, James. "The Negro Fort." Gulf Coast Historical Review 5 (Spring, 1990): 70-86.

_____. "Migration of the Seminoles into Florida," Florida Historical Quarterly 46.4 (April, 1968): 340-357.

Davis, T. Frederick. "Pioneer Florida." Florida Historical Quarterly 22.2 (October, 1943): 57-62.

_____. "The Seminole Council, October 23-25, 1834." Florida Historical Quarterly 7.4 (April, 1929): 330-350.

Denham, James M. "Some Prefer the Seminoles": Violence and Disorder among Soldiers and Settlers in the Second Seminole War, 1835–1842." Florida Historical Quarterly 70.1 (July, 1991): 38-54.

Geist, Christopher D. "Slavery among the Indians: An Overview," Negro History Bulletin 38.7 (1975): 465-467.

Granade, Ray. "Slave Unrest in Florida." Florida Historical Quarterly 55.1 (July, 1976): 18-36.

Heidler, David S. "The Politics of National Aggression: Congress and the First Seminole War." Journal of the Early Republic 13.4 (1993): 501-530.

Jarvis, Nathan S. "An Army Surgeon's Notes on Frontier Service, 1833–1848." Journal of the Military Service Institute of the United States 39: 275-86, 451-66; 40: 269-277.

Johnson, Charles Jr. "Black Seminoles: Their History and Their Quest for Land." Journal of the Afro-American Historical and Genealogical Society 1.2 (1980): 47-58.

Johnson, Michael. "Runaway Slaves and the Slave Communities in South Carolina." William and Mary Quarterly 3 (1980): 397-428.

Katz, William L. "Black and Indian Cooperation and Resistance to Slavery." Freedomways 17 (1977): 164-74.

Kilson, Marion de B. "Towards Freedom: An Analysis of Slave Revolts in the United States." Phylon 25.2 (2nd Qtr. 1964): 175-187.

Klos, George. "Blacks and the Seminole Indian Removal Debate, 1821–1835," Florida Historical Quarterly 680.1 (July, 1989): 55-78.

Koerprer, Phillip E., Childress David. "The Alabama Volunteers in the Second Seminole War." Alabama Review 37.1 (January, 1984): 3-13.

Krogman, Wilton M. "The Racial Composition of the Seminole Indians in Florida and Oklahoma." The Journal of Negro History 19.4 (October, 1934): 412-430.

Landers, Jane. "Black–Indian Interaction in Spanish Florida." Colonial Latin American Historical Review 2.2 (Spring, 1993): 141-162.

_____. "Gracia Real de Santa Teresa de Mose: A Free Black Town in Spanish Colonial Florida." American Historical Review 95.1 (February, 1990): 1-34.

Largent, Floyd B. Jr. "The Florida Quagmire." American History 34.4 (1989): 40-46.

Love, Edgan F. "Legal Restrictions on Afro-Indian Relations in Colonial Mexico." Journal of Negro History 55.2 (April, 1970): 131-139.

Meek, A.B. "The Journal of A.B. Meek and the Second Seminole War, 1836." ed. John K. Mahon, Florida Historical Quarterly 30.4 (April, 1958): 328-342.

Miller, Susan. "Seminoles and Africans under Seminole Law: Sources and Discourses of Tribal Sovereignty and 'Black Indian' Entitlement." Wicazo-Sa Review (Spring, 2005): 1-52.

154   Anthony E. Dixon

Moulton, Gary E. "Cherokees and the Second Seminole War." Florida Historical Quarterly 53.3 (January, 1975): 286-220.

Murdoch, Richard K. "The Return of Runaway Slaves 1790–1794." Florida Historical Quarterly 38.2 (October, 1959): 96-113.

Ogunleye, Tolagbe. "The Self-Emancipated Africans of Florida: Pan-African Nationalists in the 'New World.'" Journal of Black Studies 27.1 (September, 1996): 24-36.

Porter, Kenneth W. "Abraham." Phylon 2.2 (2nd Qtr., 1941): 105-116.

_____. "Davy Crockett and John Horse: A Possible Origin of the Coonskin Story." American Literature 15.1 (March, 1943): 10-15.

_____. "Early Life of Luis Pacheco." Negro History Bulletin 7.3 (December, 1943): 52-55.

_____. "Florida Slaves and Free Negroes in the Seminole War, 1835–1842." Journal of Negro History 28.4 (October, 1943): 390-421.

_____. "John Caesar: Seminole Negro Partisan." Journal of Negro History 31.2 (April, 1946): 190-207

_____. "Farewell to John Horse: An Episode of Seminole Negro Folk History." Phylon 8 (1947): 265-273.

_____. "Negro Guides and Interpreters in the Early Stages of the Second Seminole War, December 28, 1835–March 6, 1837." Journal of Negro History 35.2 (April, 1950): 174-182.

_____. "Negroes and the East Florida Annexation Plot, 1811–1813" Journal of Negro History 30.1 (January, 1945): 9-29.

_____. "Negroes and the Seminole War, 1835–1842." Journal of Southern History 30.4 (November, 1964): 427-50.

_____. "Relationships Between Negroes and Indians: Within the Present Limits of the United States." Journal of Negro History 17.3 (July, 1932): 287-367.

_____. "Seminole Flight from Marion." Florida Historical Quarterly 22.3 (January, 1944): 111-134.

_____. "Thlonoto-sassa: A Note on An Obscure Seminole Village of the Early 1820s." Florida Anthropologist 13 (December, 1960): 115-119.

_____. "The Negro Abraham." Florida Historical Quarterly 25.1 (July, 1946): 1-43.

Riordan, Patrick. "Finding Freedom in Florida: Native Peoples, African Americans, and Colonists, 1670–1816." Florida Historical Quarterly 75.7 (January, 1996): 24-43.

Rivers, Larry E. and Brown, Canter. "The Indispensable Man": John Horse and Florida's Second Seminole War." The Journal of the Georgia Association of Historians 18 (1997): 1-24.

Roberts, Albert H. "The Dade Massacre." Florida Historical Quarterly 5.3 (January, 1927): 123-138.

Roberts, Donald J. "Ambush in Florida." Military Heritage 4.4 (2003): 70-79, 88-89.

Saint, Claudio. "The English Has Now a Mind to Make Slaves of Them All": Creeks, Seminoles, and the Problem of Slavery." American Indian Quarterly 22.2 (1998): 157-180.

Siebert, Wilbur H. "Slavery and White Servitude in East Florida, 1726–1776." Florida Historical Quarterly 10.1 (July, 1931): 4-23.

Spoehr, Alexander. "Kinship System of the Seminole." Field Museum of Natural History Anthropological Series 33.2 (1941): 1-29.

Sturtevant, William C. "Creek into Seminole," in Leacock, Eleanor B., Lurie, Nancy Eds. North American Indians in Historical Perspective. New York: Random House, 1971: 188-211.

Tappan, John S. "Tallahassee and St Marks in 1841: A Letter of John S. Tappan." Ed. W.T. Cash, Florida Historical Quarterly 24.2 (October, 1945): 108-112.

Thybony, S. "Against All Odds, Black Seminoles Won Their Freedom." Smithsonian 22 (1991): 90-101.

Tidwell, John. "The Maroons." American Legacy: Magazine of African American History and Culture 8.2 (2002): 41-42, 44-47, 50.

Tucker, Phillip Thomas. "John Horse: Forgotten African-American Leader of the Second Seminole War." The Journal of Negro History 77.2. (Spring, 1992): 74-83.

Walker, Hester P. "Massacre at Indian Key, August 7, 1840, and the Death of Dr Henry Perrine." Florida Historical Quarterly 5.1 (July, 1926): 18-42.

Watts, Jill. "We Do Not Live For Ourselves Only": Seminole Black Perceptions and the Second Seminole War." UCLA Historical Journal 7 (1986): 5-28.

Welsh, Michael G. "Legislating a Homestead Bill: Thomas Hart Benton and the Second Seminole War." Florida Historical Quarterly 57.1 (July, 1978): 157-172.

White, Frank F. Ed. "A Journal of Lt Robert C Buchanan during the Seminole War (The Battle of Okeechobee)." Florida Historical Quarterly 29.2 (October, 1950): 132-151.

_____. Ed. "The Journals of Lieutenant John Pickell, 1836-1837." Florida Historical Quarterly 38.2 (October, 1959): 142-171.

_____. "Macomb's Mission to the Seminoles." Florida Historical Quarterly 35.2 (October, 1956): 130-193.

Wright, J. Leitch Jr. "A Note on the First Seminole War as Seen by the Indians, Negroes, and their British Advisors." Journal of Southern History 34.4 (November, 1968): 565-575.

Young, Capt Hugh. "A Topographical Memoir on East and West Florida with Itineraries (Continued)." Florida Historical Quarterly 13.2 (October, 1934): 82-104.

Young, Rogers W. "Fort Marion during the Seminole War, 1835-1842." Florida Historical Quarterly 13.4 (April, 1935): 193-223.

Made in the USA
Middletown, DE
29 May 2015